AF610069

HTP

Copyright © 2020 by Jonathan J. Mize

All rights reserved. No part of this book may be reproduced in any form or by an electronic or mechanical means, including information storage and retrieval systems, without permission in writing from the publisher/author, except by a reviewer who may quote brief passages in a review.

Disclaimer: This work has not yet been approved by Mr. Christopher Langan.

First paperback edition June 2020

ISBN 978-1-71683-529-2 (paperback)

Published by Holotheist Press

Dallas, TX

TRACTATUS LOGICO-SYNDIFFEONICUS

Tractatus Logico-Syndiffeonicus

Jonathan J. Mize

HOLOTHEIST PUBLICATIONS

Dallas, Texas

AN INTRODUCTION

Eccentric, *obsessed*, intellectually *fastidious*, sometimes *cryptic*; when these adjectives are uttered, it takes very little for the mind to wander towards Ludwig Wittgenstein. Though, in his later years, he turned away from the ambitious assembly of metaphysical structure, setting his sights on more "linguistically-bound" issues, the metaphysical work that he did complete still warrants great applaud and eager exegesis. Yet, it is certainly not only his productions and personality that are interesting. Wittgenstein lived in an age with a *fundamentally different* intellectual milieu than can be glimpsed today. The first edition of what is currently known as his *Tractatus Logico-Philosophicus*, then called *Logisch-Philosophische Abhandlung*, was published in the 1921 edition of the journal "Annalen der Naturphilosophie", *without a single work of reference or citation*. Although we mustn't over–idealize the time period, one cannot deny that the environment was different, more conducive, one might say, to revolutionary insight.

In this book we shall pay homage to Wittgenstein, utilizing elements of his (earlier) literary style, ultimately "throwing away" his famous ladder, straightening ourselves up to face our new destination, a profoundly novel metaphysical paradigm, that of Christopher Langan's *Cognitive-Theoretic Model of the Universe*, or **CTMU**. Certainly, it is not merely style upon which we have drawn our comparison. There is a common drive amongst the two—Wittgenstein and Langan—the drive for *Truth*, something which has become increasingly difficult to find in modern day academia. It is in our age, *this* age, that drive for Truth has been dampened in the face of peer–acceptance and staunch gate–keeping by the intellectual "in–group". No doubt, many great technical advances have resulted from the collaborative process of peer–review and the highly-specialized (though quasi–sectarian) intellectual landscape at large. However, those factors which are conducive to the development of truly *radical* and profound shifts in worldview most prominently the willingness to consider works generated from *first principle*, those which superficially and/or substantively stand apart from the rest—these factors have been hidden, drowned out by the numb roar of an intellectual bureaucracy, determined to endow each and every eager, inquisitive soul with "marketable skills", seizing his/her curiosity and money along the way.

Given these aforementioned considerations, it would come as little surprise that the theories of an autodidactic academic *outsider* such as Christopher Langan have, on the whole, not been taken too seriously. However, within the last decade or so, Langan's theory, the CTMU, has seen a burgeoning body of support. In 2017, the peer-reviewed journal "Cosmos and History" accepted his paper, "An Introduction to Mathematical Metaphysics" for publication. Then, the next year, two more of Langan's articles were published. Langan, along with the renowned physicist and author of *The Tao of Physics*, Fritjof Capra, has achieved record numbers of article downloads, per the Cosmos and History journal. In addition, in 2019, the author published a book, *God versus Language: Contrasting Metaphysical Methods of Wittgenstein's Tractatus and Langan's CTMU*, analyzing (and ultimately advancing) the theory.

This rising success notwithstanding, there is a far grander vision waiting just around the corner; the proverbial *paradigm shift* awaits. It is well understood that to invoke such a term is no light matter. All the same, the CTMU is no light theory. And before we lead the reader into the grand theoretical edifice that it is, we find it worthwhile to consider the nature of this moment in scientific and philosophical history. We will discuss some pertinent elements of recent philosophy of science, ending with some musings on the future of society, pre and post CTMU integration.

Philosophy of Science

We may start by visiting an especially prescient quote from the great J.S. Mill, taken from his *A System of Logic.*

> Most thinkers of any degree of sobriety allow, that an hypothesis...is not to be received as probably true because it accounts for all the known phenomena, since this is a condition sometimes fulfilled tolerably well by two conflicting hypotheses...while there are probably a thousand more which are equally possible, but which, for want of anything analogous in our experience, our minds are unfitted to conceive. ([1867] 1900, 328)

This is the essence of the famous Duhem–Quine thesis, i.e., that no scientific hypothesis and its predictions can be considered apart from various implicit "background" assumptions. Beneath each component—formal and observational—of any given hypothesis lies various "bundles" of concepts, all of which are susceptible to *revision*, based upon *future observation.* It is upon this basic foundation that Thomas Kuhn composed his philosophy of science. Challenging the holist, *organicist* even, philosophy of science, in which theoretical advance (and every auxiliary "fine-tuning") is a movement towards truth, Kuhn introduced (or, perhaps more accurately, eloquently portrayed) the notion of *theoretical incommensurability*. The (debatably) Kuhnian notion of theoretic incommensurability has exhibited a great variety of meanings and subtleties throughout the years, so it will behoove us to analyze the notion logically, from first principle. We will however, introduce an excerpt from the late maverick philosopher of science Paul Feyerabend's "Explanation, Reduction and Empiricism" (1962):

> The order introduced into our experiences by Newton's theory is retained and improved by relativity. This means that the concepts of relativity theory are sufficiently rich to allow us to state all the facts which were stated before with the help of Newtonian physics. Yet these two sets of categories are completely different and *bear no logical relation to each other.* (emphasis added)

This can be viewed as a direct attack on the logical positivist/empiricist notion of cumulative theoretical aggregation (what we just recently called the *holist* view), that is, the notion that each theoretical advance is a progression towards some epistemic ideal. While—to someone roughly acquainted with the CTMU's methodology (of metalogic)—it may seem that the logical empiricist stance would be CTMU-compatible, this is not exactly the case. Let us explain.

In contemporary philosophy of science, model theory is often offered as a handy formal device for the analysis of theoretical complexes. In Da Costa and French's "The Model-Theoretic Approach in the Philosophy of Science", we see an interesting approach, in which a certain scientific theory T with a given "domain of knowledge" (more on this shortly), symbolized as Δ, as analyzed as the restriction of Δ, is a so-called "partial structure" $\mathfrak{A}$,

$$\mathfrak{A} = \langle A_1, R_i \rangle_{i \in I}$$

where A_1 is the set of observable individuals of Δ, R_i, $i \in I$ is a family of partial relations defined on A_1, where I is an appropriate index set. Where a partial relation defined on a set A be simply defined as a set $\langle R_1, R_2, R_3 \rangle$, where R_1 is the set of ordered pairs which satisfy R, R_2 is the set of ordered pairs which do not satisfy R, and R_3 is the set of ordered pairs for which it is left open whether they satisfy R or not.

Although this approach may yield fair amounts of utility in terms of the analysis of specific theories, there is a fatal flaw lurking in the background of its machinery. There is an insidious injection of *Cartesian dualism* into the approach. Now, there are of course myriad different facets of said dualism, but the crux of the matter can be grokked simply by considering the so-called Cartesian coordinate system. In a given equation plotted on the coordinate system, we of course see points and their intermediate continua. What we do *not* see, however, is any sort of consideration of the relationships between the given content or attribute of points and whatever structure (model-theoretic or otherwise) necessary to sustain the interaction between these "modeled" points. The core reason why this lack of expressivity has not been lamented sooner is simply because, for all *linear* intents and purposes, the Cartesian coordinate system is a well-oiled machine; where the current state is a result of solely the relevant *preceding* states, there is no pressing need to alter the means of representation. In the CTMU, however, the current state is a product of much, much more than certain preceding states.

With this knowledge in hand, we may now move back to our originally broached notion of *theoretical incommensurability*. Feyerabend posited that incommensurable theories "are completely different and bear no logical relation to each other". Given our above discussion on the shortcomings of Cartesian dualism, this clearly depends on the "dualistic status", so to speak, of our given means of analysis. To Da Costa and French, with their structure $\mathfrak{A} = \langle A_1, R_i \rangle_{i \in I}$, the incommensurability of theories can be simply depicted, via the movement from a given domain of knowledge, Δ, to another, Δ′. This quasi-discrete "jumping" from one domain to another runs orthogonally to the positivist notion of holist accumulation of knowledge, no doubt. But is this view compatible with a CTMU-centered philosophy of science? Well, yes and no.

Moving back to the Feyerabend quote, we see that he also posits that "…the concepts of relativity theory are sufficiently rich to allow us to state all the facts which were stated before with the help of Newtonian physics." This of course applies when we are speaking of a ToE (Theory of Everything), such as the CTMU; if the CTMU did not offer an explanation of the "basic" dynamics of Newtonian physics, then it would simply not qualify as a bone fide ToE. At the same time, depending upon the *logical* expressivity of a succeeding domain of knowledge, Δ′, it need *not* be the case that Δ′ and Δ are "completely different", bearing "no logical relation to each other". The very statement *precluding* the possibility a domain Δ′ logically uniting with a domain Δ is nonsensical. Here, we reach another insidious facet of Cartesian dualism—the exclusion of all that which is ostensibly "subjective".

Where the points represented on a Cartesian coordinate system are abstracted away from any attribute, there is no possible way to even broach the analysis of such supposedly hopelessly "sticky" notions as consciousness and qualia; the points on the grid are mere representational shells of the various phenomena of the world. It is here that we reach one of Langan's most profound points of CTMU establishment—the emphasis upon the unification of language, theory and universe, symbolically, $\mathcal{L}$, T and U. Model-theoretically, Langan stresses that we must expand our universe of discourse, A, beyond a mere amorphous collection of members a_n, out into each and every *real entity* of our intelligible universe, U. In this process of the expansion of A, we discover that our universe U can not only be modeled upon a given $\mathcal{L}$ and T, but that it is indeed *itself* a language *and* a theory (and a model). We can see that this is no move of mere scientific observation; this is *metaphysics.* What does this entail for our two domains of knowledge, Δ' and Δ then? Given that the model of reality (which is also the identity of reality)—known by Langan as M—models all that is *real,* we see that if our Δ' is M, then no matter what Δ consists of, M serves as a model of it! And although it may seem rather peculiar that there is no restriction on the content of Δ, the very ability of identification (*perception*) of its members ensures that these members are real and *must be* modeled by M. This is an interesting pivot back towards the logical empiricist conception of scientific advance—advance as progression towards some epistemic ideal. Of course though, as the CTMU is metaphysics, as opposed to a scientific theory, there are a few crucial differences. The logical empiricist holist stance on scientific advance acknowledges neither the constituent system of symbols nor the factor of mental impetus (the scientist/philosopher) as entities of theoretical discussion; the canvas of experiment cares not about its composition, unfortunately.

Given the nature of the structure of the CTMU, we may call its related philosophy of science, the *supertautological stance.* We here defer to Langan, from his landmark exposition, "The Cognitive-Theoretic Model of the Universe: A New Kind of Reality Theory" in describing this term:

> First, [the CTMU] is supertautological; being constructed to mirror logical tautology up to the level of model theory and beyond, it is true in much the same way that a theory of pure mathematics would be true, but with reference to an expanded universe consisting of both mathematical and physical reality.

The CTMU is to be seen as the final model, the metalogical bedrock upon which all future scientific advances will sit atop. The supertautological stance has a very specific, refined view of scientific theories and their interrelations. We have already said that *any possible* Δ (domain of knowledge) is modeled by M (the identity of reality), but we have not yet discussed the criteria of a certain scientific *submodel* of M, say $\mathfrak{A}^M$, holding as a CTMU-compatible and informative scientific theory.

Plain and simple, for a given $\mathfrak{A}^M$ to be considered CTMU-compatible, it must take into account all of M's *syntactic invariants*. For those unfamiliar with the CTMU's use of the term "syntax", we shall defer to Langan once more, presenting an array of its uses from his 2002 exposition of the theory:

> …a syntax consisting of (a) logical and geometric rules of structure, and (b) an inductive-deductive generative grammar identifiable with the laws of state transition.
>
> As defined by this statement, the predicate reality is primarily a linguistic construct conforming to syntactic structure, where syntax consists of the rules by which predicates are constructed and interpreted. In this sense, reality amounts to a kind of theory whose axioms and rules of inference are implicitly provided by the logical component of the conceptual syntax in which it is expressed.
>
> That is, because reality requires a syntax consisting of general laws of structure and evolution, and there is nothing but reality itself to serve this purpose, reality comprises its own self-distributed syntax under MU (which characterizes the overall relationship between syntax and content).

All those syntactic elements that M holds stable, these are the criteria which must be met by $\mathfrak{A}^M$. Many syntactic elements, for example, various nomological strings or "laws of physics", vary per time slice. Those syntactic elements that are invariant are often, though certainly not always, of a level "above" the mere physical "output" domain. Foregoing any sort of deep analysis, we can simply develop a general set of invariance, Syn^{INV}. As we recently mentioned, in the CTMU, there is a three-way coincidence of (logical) theory, universe and model; this is one respect in which the theory is "trialic". Given this, for a $\mathfrak{A}^{M}$ to pass the CTMU litmus test, it must include all elements of Syn^{INV}, in its domain of discourse (or "universe" of discourse), signature (list of relevant symbols in the language L) and interpretation function *I*. Consequently, said $\mathfrak{A}^{M}$ will contain all elements of Syn^{INV} in its *theory* T and *model.* We can glimpse here what Langan terms *hology*, the property of reality, whereby the *entire* syntax of reality (all entities within), at any given time slice (both invariant and variant syntax) is "injected" into each real entity, ensuring the mutual consistency of all that is real. It may at first sound counterintuitive to consider members of signatures, domains and theories as vehicles of said syntax, but, once one gets the hang of this, its efficiency (not to mention *necessity*) becomes quite apparent. Where a simplified potential signature of a given $\mathfrak{A}^{M}$ consists of a set *S* of function and relation symbols, we can construct a simple example for maximal intellectual uptake.

Let's say that we have certain "quanta" of mental entities, say, cognitions, qualia and perceptions (taken from the author's "A Novel Semantics for Belief, Knowledge and Psychological Alethic Modality" (2020)). We can symbolize these as p, q and g. We can view a function of these quanta as a "volitionary function", reflecting upon and subsequently acting upon the current mental state. In the process of said "reflection", various volitionary functions act upon (take as argument) myriad arrangements of previous quanta; we may abstract these arrangements as simple relations of quanta, say pRg and qRp. A given volitionary function, f_v will then look something like, $f_v(pRg) = x$ with the output being any arbitrary chain of quanta.

In talking about various logical elements of the mind, we reach the Langanian notion of HCS or "Human Cognitive-Perceptual Syntax". Given that reality is fundamentally *generative*, that is, logico-linguistic in nature, it is apparent that there must be specific rules of operation and conjugacy corresponding to the various facets of the mind and brain. For all volitionary functions and all quanta, it is necessary that the rules of operation of reality as a whole are somehow "recognizable", so that both (a) M can recognize these symbols, considering them and placing them in their proper places and (b) these symbols retain coherency, staying stable throughout the evolution of reality. Here's more on the latter component, from Langan's "Introduction to Quantum Metamechanics (QMM)":

> The coherence of a symbol is what enables it to have a definite meaning and to be treated as a single unified entity. The coherence property is crucial; it means that anything possessing it can be treated as a unitary entity which behaves or transforms in a unified and regular way under certain mathematical or physical operations. Defined in terms of the coherence property, [formal quantization] means "division of a coherent identity into coherent subidentities which act as unitary entities and thus behave coherently."

In terms of HCS, the volitionary functions f_v and relations between quanta, R must contain the rules of operation and conjugacy for all other varied elements of cognitive syntax, in order for such formal coherency to transpire. This is a "miniature" example of Langan's hology at work in the signature of reality; hology outright is the principle that each and every real entity contains the rules of operation of M, the identity of reality.

Back to the model-theoretic properties of reality and the accompanying philosophy of science of the supertautological stance. Although it is true that the CTMU forces an expansion of all given domains of knowledge, Δ, this expansion—contra Da Costa and French's approach in their exposition of model-theoretic philosophy of science—is such that the new domain, U, the collection of all real entities, is part and parcel of a reality-theoretic, *self-modeling* entity, M. Thus, M is the reality-theoretic canonical model of reality. Where scientific theories sufficiently conform to the structure of M, we can once again pick up what the logical empiricists thought to be so somberly lost—the view of scientific advancement as progression towards an (The) epistemic ideal.

A Metaformally-Informed Society

The shift in conceptualization and theorization associated with the CTMU can essentially be seen as the world's first *metaphysical* paradigm shift. This is of course not to say that there have been no previous shifts in worldview, rather, it is the case that no previous shift in worldview has been the result of logically-buttressed metaphysical insight. Scientific paradigm shifts, for all their utility, rarely have impact upon the configurations of *society* as a whole. Even further, scientific paradigm shifts rarely have impact upon the *ethical* frameworks of the world. The metaphysical paradigm shift is a new beast, and its societal import is profound. The core of the societal impact deals with the age-old collectivism | individualism dichotomy. Many great thinkers have wrestled with this dualism, spawning various ostensible solutions. Perhaps the most philosophically known "solution" was presented by the philosopher of science Karl Popper, in his two-volume tome *The Open Society and Its Enemies* (1945). Popper utilizes a tetrapartite conceptual distinction between *individualism, collectivism*, *altruism* and *egoism.* Glossing over the economic sense of these terms, Popper homes in on their cultural, political and ethical senses. He claimed that altruism need not be in coupling with collectivism, and that a primarily individualist society can indeed promote and value altruism. Given the internationally-contentious time in which *The Open Society* was written, it is certainly understandable that Popper should take such staunch opposition to collectivism, however, in our current age, at the doorstep of a metaphysical paradigm shift, we have no lasting reason to demonize collectivism. That being said, both collectivism and individualism proper, in their current forms, are inadequate for a CTMU-informed society.

In Langan's 2018 essay, "Metareligion as the Human Singularity", he reaches down into the core of the collectivism | individualism dichotomy:

> The Human and Tech Singularities relate to each other by a kind of duality; the former is extended and spacelike, representing the even distribution of spiritual and intellectual resources over the

whole of mankind, while the latter is a compact, pointlike concentration of all resources in the hands of just those who can afford full access to the best and most advanced technology. Being opposed to each other with respect to the distribution of the resources of social evolution, they are also opposed with respect to the structure of society; symmetric distribution of the capacity for effective governance corresponds to a social order based on individual freedom and responsibility, while extreme concentration of the means of governance leads to a centralized, hive-like system at the center of which resides an oligarchic concentration of wealth and power, with increasing scarcity elsewhere due to the addictive, self-reinforcing nature of privilege.

At the time Popper wrote his *Open Society*, there was no viable ToE, no metaphysical arbiter of Truth. Thus, without a guiding framework under which to place ethics and virtue, individualism seemed the "safe" route to go. Unfortunately, though such individualism may be "safer" in the sense that it wards off infectious forms of nationalism and collectivism (fascism, socialism and communism), it is ultimately none the better in terms of ethical orientation. In a society teeming with strong and "independent" individuals, each striving to make his/her own "destiny", what is forgone is the potential of a deep spiritual and metaphysical connection amongst all, transcending the boundaries of the individuals and orienting their goals, desires and wills towards Truth. Karl Popper was warry of such a program, largely because he saw no possible metaphysical truth worthy of serving as (The) Truth; he made himself content with so-called "piecemeal social engineering", the incessant oppositional tinkering against ostensible *evils*, neglecting as best as possible any potential collective, orienting *good* (and especially any sort of Good). In Popper's proclamation that "history has no meaning", we find a strident, near sacrilegious chord, clashing with the CTMU's conception of teleology. In Langanian metaphysics, the current moment in history is not a mere notch on some blandly-colored ruler; each and every moment is the result of an entire metaphysical symphony, with the efforts of each and every denizen of reality combining to produce what can either be a moment "better" than before (or after) or one "worse" than before (or after). And, where we have a logico-mathematical conception of free-will, we can (freely!) feel even more empowered to synthesize a harmonious string of historical moments.

Nonetheless, many—especially those unacquainted with the specifics of Langan's work—likely still have trouble seeing how such an ostensibly "dry" and abstract framework can imbue spiritual and ethical life into the world. "Wouldn't it be easier to continue preaching for empathy and faith?", it might be retorted. Although this is largely an understandable reaction from those who are CTMU-unacquainted, we can confidently present an example of philosophy's perhaps surprisingly deep and plumbing reach into society, so as to inspire the imagination towards a metaformally-informed society. The notions of *natural law* and *natural right* are prime examples of "mere philosophical" concepts that have had a resounding impact upon the construction of society and its ethical pipelines. In the age in which these notions were first generated, it is all too likely that their progenitors faced such criticisms as "why is this necessary? why can't we just have more faith in our *destinies*?" were incessantly proffered, despite continuous rational argument thereagainst. This example falls under a broad and longstanding cultural, perhaps even *human* paradigm, that of personal versus societal teleology. Of course, the simple personal | societal dichotomy is nowhere near the whole of the battle; there is much subtlety to be found. Here it may be a helpful heuristic to employ the distinction between deep and shallow teleology, where "teleology" is construed in a very loose sense, roughly synonymous with goal-orientation. Without painting with too broad of a brush, we can safely say that a fair number of people take the stance of *shallow personal teleology*, i.e., the view that one should not try to concoct plans to reach and change society, as it is ultimately up to the preference of the individual, and such schemes are fruitless. Far from a heartily constructed and expertly defended position, the stance of shallow personal teleology is often taken up by those who have little care or ability to think abstractly, about society as an entity (although, as we will see shortly, academic stances of this sort *do* exist).

The above retorts,

"Wouldn't it be easier to continue preaching for empathy and faith?"

and

"why is this necessary? why can't we just have more faith in our *destinies*?",

these are prime examples of the shallow personal teleology stance; to this group, those who try and run against the societal current are as good as mentally insane. Contrasting with this then, a stance of *deep personal teleology* is roughly the view that although attempts to run against the currents of society are not necessarily fruitless, the ultimate guiding-goal of such a project should, first and foremost (perhaps to the exclusion of consideration of more collectively-oriented goals) be to endow the *individual* with more "utility" (however this may be construed) than before. Now, one might be tempted to draw a direct link between such a "deep personal teleologist" and a Popperian "piecemeal social engineer", but this would be misguided. To further solidify the distinction, we should emphasize the accompanying *means* of societal alteration of which we can speak. In the Popperian sense, in the "piecemeal" sense, we have what may be called a practical or *intra-paradigmatic* sense of societal alteration in mind. That is, to Popper, it would be unwise to do *either* (a) attempt to break the bounds of the current societal worldview, as buttressed ostensibly firmly by individual rights and bureaucratic institutions and values or (b) apply the results of such a paradigmatic breakage to the workings of society as a whole. Such an approach would be considered a prime example of grandiose "holistic social engineering" by Popper. With this, we see that Popper's piecemeal social engineering does not even meet the criteria of a deep personal teleological stance on societal change. This method is of a *shallow personal teleological* nature, however sophisticated it may sound. As the complexity of our terms is now proliferating, we wish to show a helpful chart here:

Stance on Societal Alteration	**Conceptual Nature of Stance**
Shallow personal teleology	*Intra-paradigmatic*
Deep personal teleology	*Intra-paradigmatic | Extra-paradigmatic*
Shallow societal teleology	*Intra-paradigmatic*
Deep societal teleology	*Intra-paradigmatic | Extra-paradigmatic*

Homing in on the last row now, the stance of *deep societal teleology*, we must demarcate a few more aspects involved. The case can certainly be made that communism was a member of the stance of the final row. So what then is the difference between this noxious ideology and the CTMU-informed human singularity? Well, to answer this fully, we must see in what manner various senses of the notion of "paradigm" play a role in the nature of the two scenarios. Communism, drawing its prime philosophical motivation from Marx's socio-historical theory of dialectical materialism, was fundamentally built upon socio-metaphysical ground, this much is evident. However, it is crucial that we ask specific questions about both (a) how this theoretical ground was (or wasn't) utilized, in the socio-political movement itself and (b) the extent to which both Hegelian dialectical idealism and Marxian dialectical materialism are suitable for the mass alteration of society. For reasons of concision, we will focus on the latter, contrasting the metaphysical import with that of the CTMU.

Any sort of ostensible paradigm shift that Marx's dialectical materialism introduced into the social sphere was quite clearly rather culturally weak. In the day-to-day operation of a communist country, the impact of the metaphysical nature of the dialectic was negligible. Should it not be the case that a genuine metaphysical paradigm shift should factor into the intermeshings of the new society, whether explicitly or implicitly? Unfortunately, although within the theory itself, a great deal of personal and social "awakening" was promised, the largest resultant societal change was that of the economic system; the overarching, quotidian routines and collective goals remained variations around the (post-imperial) societal norm. But, even more, for all dialectical idealism's ostensible intuitiveness and aesthetic appeal, it does not rest upon a logically-firm ground. Even if it were given a "rigorous", axiomatic structure—as is actually attempted in a category-theoretic manner by so-called "post-Marxist" philosopher Alain Badiou—it would not attain status as a theory based upon *irrefutability*. The order of irrefutability is indeed the tallest order that can possibly be requested; it is the fact that no theory *in the history of the world* has yet attained such status. We could even make the following claim, drawing back to Popper and his take: if a staunch defender of the Popperian "piecemeal social engineering" approach were to see *irrefutable* proof of a given metaphysical system, then this said defender, if he were anything short of mentally unstable, would sacrifice his original views, yielding to what cannot be denied. Unfortunately, throughout the centuries, as philosophical framework after philosophical framework failed to yield little more than intriguing (though perhaps aesthetically inspiring) conjecture, the intellectual community's hope and longing for Truth dwindled. Today, sadly, it seems near offensive to consider something to be irrefutable. Although one not familiar with the CTMU is of course not expected to take our assertion here at face value, we can provide some brief insight into the deep logical nature of the theory. This excerpt below is taken from the author's *God versus Language*.

> The CTMU—moving from the particular to the general and the to the extension thereof—utilizes a form of *inductive* reasoning…the CTMU utilizes the {(*known*) $\rightarrow_u$ (*known/unknown*)} inductive template…[We] can see how Langanian induction differs from orthodox induction—by virtue of it transforming a traditional inducitve {(*known*) $\rightarrow_u$ (*known/unknown*)} reasoning structure into a {(*known*) $\rightarrow_\square$ (*extensionofknown*)} structure of induction by logical

necessity. Obviating a deductive "turtles all the way down" infinite string of axioms, Langan has both engineered a novel variety of reasoning and, more importantly, utilized this novel construction to prove the existence of a Higher Being or Creator. To reach this ultimate conclusion he coupled the structure *P*, $\{((existence) \wedge (perception)) \rightarrow_{\Box} (necess.prop.ofReality)\}$, with the form $\{(known) \rightarrow_{u} (structureofReality)\}$, yielding $\{(P) \rightarrow_{\Box} (structureofReality)\}$. The trick lay in turning the traditional, consequence relation of uncertainty, '$\rightarrow_{u}$', into one of logical necessity '$\rightarrow_{\Box}$'.

Once this knowledge of irrefutable metaphysical Truth is thoroughly disseminated throughout society, we will be in a position to obsolete each aforementioned "stance on societal alteration"; society will need no more extra-paradigmatic reaching, and all "alteration" will be translated into *progression*, societal and ethical progression towards the ideal of M. This will be an entirely new epoch for humanity.

Tractatus Logico-Syndiffeonicus

"In the beginning was the Word, and the Word was with God, and the Word was God."

—John 1:1

A Few Remarks

Though the concepts have changed, there remains a mysterious similarity; there is a redolence here, as in Wittgenstein's Tractatus, of a drawing of philosophical, conceptual ends. Wittgenstein—in both continuously mentioning and ostensibly rebutting his contemporary, Bertrand Russell's notions—attempted to shift the entire disciplines of logic and metaphysics behind the vanguard that was Tractarian thought. But, as brilliant as he may have been, Wittgenstein, in holding fast to his logical-representational method, was forced to advance cryptic, exegesis-requiring remarks, shying away from firm, implicative substance. Yet, it would be foolish to intimate that Wittgenstein himself did not feel a visceral, moving sense of certainty in his conclusions. Indeed, it would be similarly foolish to assert that the philosophical community, in its reception and, often, befuddlement, viewed his work as a mere collection of nebulous, imprecise remarks. Wittgenstein, in constructing such a subtlety-laden, profound work, essentially carved his name into the list of greats, regardless of the Tractatus's historical reception. Indeed, here we intend to bring about something quite similar—this time for a man named Christopher Langan—with, however, an extremely important caveat: Langan, in his CTMU, has *logically immunized* the theory from subsequent corruption or rebuttal; it is the essence of the *supertautology* that is his reality theory. Here, in displaying the guts of the CTMU for all to see, we hope to help cement its place into philosophical and societal preeminence. Nonetheless, just as Wittgenstein addressed various 'competing' notions of his day, we will here find it pertinent to address various metaphysical approaches and programs along the way, illustrating how they can be subsumed under the CTMU. And, in the end, it is hoped that the reader may at last receive the sheer pleasure of climbing a stratospheric intellectual ladder and *remain atop*, for all to see.

1 That which can be linguistically referenced is all that is the case, that which is *real.*

1.1 More so than this, the means of reference and the various functions thereof can be themselves linguistically referenced and are thus themselves *real.*

1.11 Another level deeper then, there cannot be a function of reference—whether descriptive, definitive, compositional, attributive, nomological or interpretative—*outside of reality*, for this would amount to this item being *unreferenceable.*

1.12 If something is purportedly unreferenceable, then this amounts to asserting a difference between this something and language or linguistic referenceability.

1.13 In asserting that something differs from linguistic referenceability, we have the relation xRy, as both the 'something' in question and the attribute of linguistic referenceability are themselves *linguistically referenceable* and thus real.

1.14 Given that something, though purported to be unreferenceable, can in fact be linguistically referenced entails that if 'something' genuinely is unreferenceable, we cannot make any claims about it whatsoever. In the words of Wittgenstein then, "What we cannot speak about we must pass over in silence."

1.15 Here we reach the principle of syndiffeonesis: whenever we assert something of the form xRy, where the 'R' is construed in the broadest manner possible, we see that there is a syntactic ontological medium enveloping both x and y, and indeed R itself. We will call the operation producing said medium of x and y the unisect, rendering it as the symbol ᘎ.

1.2 When we consider the dualism of Kant and Descartes, the chasm between the phenomenal and the noumenal, we see that the noumena, being linguistically referenceable, and standing in a difference relationship to the mind, can be included in an expression of the form $p \cup\!\cap n$.

1.3 Having determined that 'noumena' are not irreducibly separated from the phenomenal realm, we can state something interesting about this dynamic. Construing the 'external world' as some sum, (noumenal + phenomenal), we can then ponder on the mind's relation to such 'external world'. We can see that the mind must be in a relationship (*mind*) $\cup\!\cap$ (*external world*), as both the mind and the external world can both (a) be linguistically referenced and (b) be (necessarily) construed as members of reality.

1.31 Given that any two things x and y that can be both (a) linguistically referenced and (b) thus be considered *real*, can be expressed as $x \cup\!\cap y$, this entails that we are permitted such expressions as $x \cup\!\cap$ *Reality*.

1.312 The essence of self-containment avails itself when we consider that the underlying ontological medium of $x \cup\!\cap$ *Reality* is simply Reality itself.

1.313 However,when considering conventional set theory (ZF), we find that a set cannot contain itself, but this is simply a feature of mathematics; it has no ontological import.

2 There are two varieties of containment—topological and descriptive. Conventional set theory is predicated upon *topological containment* only. By topological containment we mean containment that can be rendered *spatially*. When simply referring to the 'boundaries' of static collections, as opposed to their definitions or natures of being, we are utilizing this topological containment. If we wish to describe the manner of existence of an object that *invokes a collection or another object in its definition*, then we must utilize descriptive containment.

2.1 Indeed to obviate the paradox that would ensue if we were to found our metaphysics upon sets equipped with only a relation of *topological* containment, we must render a theory of real-predicated objects immune to infinite regress of containment. It is clear that, for this, we must utilize *descriptive* containment.

2.11 In constructing a theory of sets equipped with both senses of containment, we find that we reach a point at which scale becomes *internally indistinguishable.* To see why this is the case we need only examine what occurs with each introduction of a superset. Say we have a set of real-predicated things, *X*, such that 'realness' is defined upon the membership of set *X* and reality is defined upon all real contents of the set *X*. Let's say that we introduce a superset of this set, *X'*. For *X*, all of its contents, in their definitions, rely upon *X*, as they are related in descriptive-containment terms to *X*. For the contents of *X*, there is *no boundary* of *X*, as it represents their definitional and descriptive *identity*. Thus, in introducing a superset *X'*, *X* will *descriptively* contain *X'*, just as *X'* will then of course topologically contain its contents (all the contents descriptively contained by *X*), as was the case with *X*. This dynamic allows the identity of reality to retain its privileged spot, not subjected to the whim of a topologico-contentively changing universe.

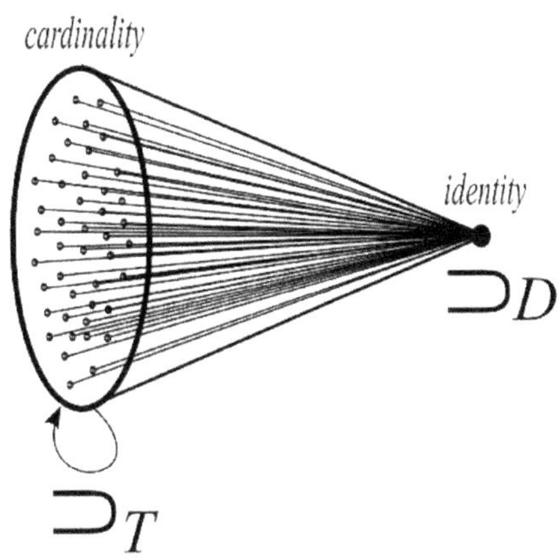

2.12 From the above, there may seem to be an additional paradox. One might object that this leaves our theory of sets open to infinite regress of topological extension (that we could have an arbitrary number of superset X's). But it must be stressed that these sets are *extensional* in nature. The identity of reality, on the other hand, is *intensional* (though of course it has extensional *aspects*). Since in this case both (a) the intensional provides the structure (rules) for the extensional, and (b) the intensional is necessarily internally consistent, we know it is the case that the extensional is *immunized from paradox*.

2.2 Duality is an essential notion for reality theory. Duality allows us to see how things behave when their structural semantics are inverted, thus allowing us to determine their structural boundaries.

2.21 Mutual definition is an important, and *necessary*, result of dualization. For example, in modal logic, the neccessity operator $\Box$ and the possibility operator $\Diamond$ are duals of one another, as $\neg p \leftrightarrow \Diamond p$ and $\neg \Diamond \neg p \leftrightarrow \Box p$. Both operators can thus be defined *mutually*.

2.22 Here, with the notion of the dual, we can see an additional potential paradox—that of an infinite nesting of duality. We of course must address the question: what is the dual of reality itself? In other words, what can reality be mutually defined with respect to? The infinite regress of powersets was 'solved' by the introduction of a novel variety of containment, but surely we cannot utilize that notion for this issue, as there is no distinct mapping between duality and extensional set theory. Indeed, we cannot simply invoke a notion of containment to sweep up duality into its secure bosom. We mentioned earlier that the identity of reality is, indeed, by definition, *intensional.* In other words, reality is not simply a collection that can be manipulated by altering its contents; it is rather a self-turned, logically idempotent self-definition. By the principle of syndiffeonesis, we can see that the dual of reality would, in being itself linguistically referenceable and thus *real*, fall under the very *same identity* as its dual. The identity of reality then, can best be informally described as the static, invariant boundary of that which is real. This, in turn, means that reality is its own dual.

2.23 Pondering more upon the nature of the boundary of that which is real, we realize that it may sound curious to assert a boundary for that which must be self-inclusive (due to syndiffeonesis). This must be a very oddly behaving boundary indeed; it must be a boundary with no real externalities.

2.3 Given that all that can be linguistically referenced is real, does the converse hold? Can all that is real be linguistically referenced? The answer to this converse turns out to be far more subtle than expected. This will be revisited soon enough, but for now the reader should be content to know the following: there are 'things' that exist purely as potentials, within a realm devoid of constraint. The existence of such 'items' can be logically proven.

2.4 It is a priori impossible that the universe is expanding, as such an expansion would entail that reality (something) was moving 'into' nothing (non-reality), thus violating the principle of syndiffeonesis $(\forall x \forall y\ (xRy)\ [x \Cup y])$.

2.41 One might however object to the above by setting up the following scenario. Why say that the space outside the universe is not a part of reality? We could in fact have a portion of reality in complete stasis 'outside' the observable universe, an ontological medium through which our observable universe expands, could we not? And what's to say that this ontological medium does not extend on infinitely?

2.42 With the above objection, one is neglecting a crucial point- this medium outside of the expanding universe falls prey to the very same powerset dilemma we have previously discussed. It is perfectly fine that there exists a ontological medium outside of the observable universe; this is not what we object to. The issue lies in the accompanying issue of either (a) where this medium would end, thus not only terminating all expansion, but more importantly violating the principle of syndiffeonesis or (b) how exactly this medium would 'adjust itself', on the fly, to possible powerset expansions. Option (a) is *a priori* impossible, as any proposed 'end point' of said medium would include a (*something*) ɰ (*nothing*) syndiffeonic relation, reducing then to a (*something*) ɰ (*something*) relation. And, as far as option (b), we have seen that the answer to such a dilemma is the very same answer we have proposed— introduce another form of containment, *descriptive* containment.

2.43 If the universe cannot, *a priori*, be expanding then why does it appear as such? We know that the universe must be size invariant, but this, we see, does not rule out a *contraction* of its contents. The contents of the universe must be shrinking at a uniform rate, so as to give, from an observer's standpoint, the *appearance* of expansion.

2.44 The universe appears to be *acceleratively* expanding because its contents are shrinking at a *constant* rate, as the ratio of content-universe size continuously *decreases* in tandem. On the other hand, if the universe itself were continuously shrinking, in tandem with its contents, the expansion would appear to be constant, not accelerating. But with such a shrinking universe, we run into an issue that ends up being the simple inverse of that of an expanding universe; the principle of syndiffeonesis is violated. For example then, say the universe were 100 units in 'size', up to its boundary, and then say that the rate of shrinkage of the universe were .87 (time- independently). We would have the sequence: [100/100 → 87/100 → 75.69/100 → …]. At each x where x/y, the observer, and all .87 of his scaled world—encapsulated by the number x—are reduced in size. One can imagine this scenario better by envisioning the contents of the observable universe as a collection of objects and the invariant 'size' thereof as a delimiting circle around them, where, one by one, a continuous proportion of objects are taken away, acceleratively closing in upon the final object.

2.5 When thinking about duality, sets and abstract process, we find that there is a particular duality relating to the dynamic evolution of reality—we may call this *constructive-filtrative duality*. Where objects or sets thereof are 'added' into reality, there is a dual process of 'subtraction' or 'filtration' of ontological potential. The specifics of such a process however will have to be addressed later.

2.51 The primary duality in terms of reality theory is that of state-syntax. Here we take "syntax" in a far broader sense than it is conventionally construed. We may, *prima facie*, view syntax as residing, at the broadest of levels, in three main classes, (a) the class of physical syntax, (b) the class of mental syntax, and (c) the class of metaphysical syntax. We can view 'states' then as any set comprising objects of, or defining each of, the three aforementioned classes. Here we have a list of dual relationships exhibited by both state and syntax: {(*objects require syntax*) ←→ (*syntax requires objects*)}, {(*objects interact with syntax*) ←→ (*syntax interacts with objects*)}, {(*objects dynamically transform to other objects via syntax*) ←→ (*syntax transforms to other syntax via objects*)}. Duality is of course a concept derived from the formal science of mathematics. A more formalized notion of the aforementioned relationships then could look something like the following: $[oRs^* = sRo]$, $[(s(i){:}\ o)^* = (o(i){:}\ s)]$, $[(s(t){:}\ o_1 \rightarrow o_2)^* = (o(t){:}\ s_1 \rightarrow s_2)]$; where * signifies the operation of dualization.

2.52 Syntax, when taken simply as the rules by which real- predicated things abide, is necessarily stratified; that is, there are numerous levels of, and purposes of, syntax.

2.53 Where syntax exists within a reality exhibiting metaphysical hierarchy, as it most certainly does, with each step up the 'ladder of abstraction', one can see that 'lower-level' strings of syntax are taken as parameters in higher-level syntactic relationships. This said ladder extends all the way up until we reach the identity of reality, the paradoxical peak without a summit that is invariant and idempotent with respect to logical operation and 'explanation'.

2.54 An identity can be informally described as a relation of equivalence $X = Y$ such that there exist variables with both X and Y such that—no matter the interpretation of the variables—X and Y generate the same result as one another. But what then do we mean by identity in the case of reality? We should begin by introducing the *model-theoretic* 'duality' of *universe* and *theory*. The universe or domain of discourse is simply a set over which the variables of the given formal language in question may range, while a theory, though its exact definition can vary, can simply be considered the set of all sentences without free variables. Where reality is self- generating (from the principle of syndiffeonesis and the neccessity of conspansion), and where higher-level syntax takes various lower-levels of syntax as parameters in conjunction with dual notions of containment, descriptive and topological, members of the universe of discourse of reality double as members of the theory or *syntax* of reality. As opposed to the dynamic of conventional model theory, where members of the universe are not directly implicated/referenced in the theory, that of CTMU-informed model-theory grants certain members of the universe a special place within the theory of reality at large; members of the universe possessing sufficient organizational complexity are directly implicated in sentences contained within the theory of reality. Depending on the stratum of syntax in question, these can either be 'types' or 'tokens' of said members.

2.55 The philosophically and logically ubiquitous phrase "syntax versus semantics", though conventionally presented as a most abstract and general dichotomy, is actually, upon closer inspection, ambiguous. In philosophical-logical parlance, syntax is a catch-all term used to signify anything and everything that is not directly related to meaning. For instance, the rules of assembly of and transformation between well-formed propositions are considered to be strictly syntactic matters. Semantic matters, then, are related to functions of truth and falsity, among various different possible interpretation functions and dynamics thereof. When we contrast this syntax-semantics heuristical divide with the reality-theoretic divide of syntax-state, we begin to see the lack of 'semantic' integration of the former. Say we are analyzing the form of a certain proposition, $x \supset y$. Adhering to the syntax-semantics dichotomy, the 'well-formedness' exhibited by the proposition, as it is rendered currently, is strictly a *syntactic* matter. Yet, when our scope of investigation is expanded, and theory is united with universe (in the model- theoretic sense), we begin to see a rich dynamic of syntax-state at play in even the ostensibly most straightforward cases. Expanding our scope to the dynamics of the mind, in the apprehension of the proposition $x \supset y$, each symbol comprising it can be taken as a 'passive' state, 'input' into the observer's mind as he/she reads it. The workings of the mind, in such a case, serve as the *syntax* in the 'construction' of the *meaning* of the proposition. This is of course not to say that the syntactic characteristics of the proposition are overridden by the mind in any sense; rather, we are simply giving an example of a parallel process, a necessary contributing factor to the observation/recognition of the syntactic qualities of $x \supset y$. Later we will see that this mental level of contributing syntax is one of many various metaphysical-syntactic layers at work within reality.

2.56 The so-called "combination problem" plaguing panpsychism is a prime example of a misapprehension, or perhaps an overextension of the syntax-semantics duality. The essence of the problem is this: where the combination problem is stated as a question of how an aggregate of merely 'mildly aware' entities gives rise to us 'more aware' entities, the issue is that the aggregation of the former entities is construed as a summing of *semantic* properties, with the accompanying question of what sort of *syntax* adheres to this sum, thus creating a *semantic* property of a 'higher level'. On the other hand, the question that eager panpsychists should be asking is this—what is the sort of metaphysical syntax that adheres to some entities, producing a *syntax-semantic* combination of a certain sort ('low-level' consciousness), while in turn both (a) adhering to other entities, producing a *syntax-semantic* combination of another sort ('higher-level' consciousness) and (b) permitting these latter entities to be composed of the former entities?

2.57 The application of the syntax-semantics duality to the above issue is permitted by the simple dynamic of conceptualization. That is, the philosophers in question of course do not utilize the syntax-semantics duality in their analysis of panpsychism, but they are unwittingly drawing upon the divide, in emphasizing certain aspects of thought and neglecting others. For instance, in thinking about a certain dynamic, with a certain interpretation, one is implicitly drawing upon the 'semantic' portion of the duality; and, on the other hand, when one thinks about a certain dynamic *solely* in terms of its rules of construction and concatenation, one is drawing upon the 'syntax' portion of the duality. Therefore, when one proclaims that there is a fundamental problem relating to the dynamic of entities given the interpretation of low-level consciousness, and the rules of metaphysics via which said entities are aggregatively summed to a certain dynamic of entities given the interpretation of higher-level consciousness, one is relying heavily upon the syntax-semantics distinction.

2.6 Chalmers's assertion that philosophical zombies are logically possible and that the notion of such is conceptually coherent is, in reality-theoretic terms (if not in other terms), misguided. The issue lies in his construal of logical possibility. In essence, his notion of logical possibility is aligned with Kant's notion of the analytic judgement; if there is no 'internal contradiction' of terms and if the possibility of the instance can be given without treading into synthetic territory, then said instance is seen as logically possible or "conceivable". While there are many contemporary philosophers who object to such an argument, on the grounds that one cannot strictly determine metaphysical matters via a simple epistemic criterion, such objections still fail to penetrate to the core of the issue. We can indeed, via the *epistemic givens* of perception and existence, delimit the boundary of logical possibility. At the same time, however, logical possibility a la Langan is a much richer notion than such an analytic-based conceivability. In fact, Langan's "logical possibility" is actually a metaphysical possibility, *induced* via *given* aspects of reality. Instead of relying upon axioms simply taken to be true, as one would in a deductive system, Langan utilizes a novel form of induction, based upon inference by logico-metaphysical neccessity. Starting from the givens that are *existence* and *perception*, he arrives at the necessary properties of reality that must hold, in order that said givens are stable and coherent; no axioms required. Then, building upon these necessary properties(logical consistency, metaphysical closure, etc.) he attains the structure of reality at large. Symbolically:

$\{((existence) \wedge (perception)) \rightarrow_{\square} (necess.prop.ofReality)\}$,

with the form

$\{(known) \rightarrow_{u} (structureofReality)\}$,

yielding

$\{(P) \rightarrow_{\square} (structureofReality)\}$,

where *P* represents the initial proposition of [((*existence*) ∧ (*perception*))..].

2.7 Gödel's famed incompleteness result—as an ostensible 'rebuttal' to the metaphysics of the CTMU—instead of being a result of a misapprehension of the syntax-semantics duality, is actually a simple case of the neglect of the hierarchy or 'nestedness' of logic and mathematics. For example, given a specific member of a given domain or "universe" of discourse, say, c_5, we can have a *metavariable*, c_x, referring to all *c*s of a certain class or designation; additionally, we can have a metavariable *c* referring to all *c*s, regardless of class or designation, and even further then, we can have a metavariable *A* referring to any given member of the universe of discourse in question. We quote a portion of Gödel's assertion below, going on the give a brief summary of its construction.

1. A *proof* for Neg (17 Gen *r*).

2. For any given *n*, for $Sb\left(r\,{}^{17}_{Z(n)}\right)$, i.e. a formal decision of 17 Gen *r* would lead to the effective demonstrability of an *ω*-inconsistency.

By the "17" in the equation, Gödel is simply referring to a given variable assigned the prime number 17, as every variable in his system is 'assigned' a distinct prime number greater than 12. By *ω*-inconsistency, Gödel means for a class of formulae *c*, and where Flg (*c*) is the smallest set of formulae that contains all the *formulae* of *c* and all axioms, and that is closed with respect to the defined relation *immediate consequence of*. Precisely, *c* is d *ω*-inconsistent if there is exists a class-sign *a* such that:

$$(n)\left[Sb\left(a\,{}^{v}_{Z(n)}\right) \in Flg\,(c)\right] \&\ [Neg\ (v\ Gen\ a)] \in Flg\,(c)$$

where v is a free variable of the class-sign a.

What Gödel finds is that one of his defined relations, the relation Bew (x), which asserts that x is a provable formula,

cannot be asserted to be recursive, ultimately serving as the catalyst for undecidability. For all the 46 relations that Gödel painstakingly defined, he put forth the proposition that for any combination of every one of these relations, $R\ (x_1 \ldots x_n)$ there is both a proof for a given substitution (Sb) and a proof of the negation (Neg) of that substitution, so that the system is both *refutation complete* and strong complete. He goes on to define the recursive relation

$$Q(x, y) = x\ Bc\left[Sb\left(y\ {}^{19}_{Z(y)}\right)\right];$$

here Bc references a previously stated relation (of the full 46 explicated) entailing that where xBy x is a proof of y. He then gives two metalinguistic 'propositions':

$$Q(x, y) \rightarrow Bew_c\left[Sb\left(q\ {}^{17}_{Z(x)}\ {}^{19}_{Z(y)}\right)\right]$$

$$Q(x, y) \rightarrow Bew_c\left[Neg\ Sb\left(q\ {}^{17}_{Z(x)}\ {}^{19}_{Z(y)}\right)\right]$$

Then, setting the class-sign p with the free variable 19 equal to 17 Gen q—or in contemporary (yet naïve) notation, V x (17(x)) [q(x)]—and thus rendering the members of q as relations implicating the free variable 19, and additionally defining the recursive class-sign r

with the free variable 17 as$Sb\left(q\ {}^{19}_{Z(p)}\right)$, we then reach the following equivalence:

$$Sb\left(q\ {}^{19}_{Z(p)}\right) = Sb\left([17\ Gen\ q]\ {}^{19}_{Z(p)}\right) = 17\ Gen\ Sb\left(q\ {}^{19}_{Z(p)}\right)$$

= 17 Gen r

Finally then, bracing for the earth-shattering result,

Gödel substitutes p for y in $xBcy$ ($Q(x,y)$), yielding:

$$\left[Sb\left(q\,{}^{17}_{Z(x)}\,{}^{19}_{Z(y)}\right)\right] = \left[Neg\ Sb\left(r\,{}^{17}_{Z(x)}\right)\right],$$

because $r = Sb\left(q\,{}^{19}_{Z(p)}\right)$

$$Q(x, 17\ \text{Gen}\ r) \rightarrow Bew_c\left[Sb\left(r\,{}^{17}_{Z(x)}\right)\right]$$

$$Q(x, 17\ \text{Gen}\ r) \rightarrow Bew_c\left[Neg\ Sb\left(r\,{}^{17}_{Z(x)}\right)\right]$$

So then, if 17 Gen r were in fact c-provable (Bew_c), there would be an n such that nB_c(17 Gen r) (from the equivalence $Bew_c(x) \equiv (Ey)\, y\, B_c\, x$), thus resulting in Neg Sb. But, at the same time, there would of course be Sb, as there exists an n for $Z(n)$.

2.71 Both of the following can be metalinguistically 'packaged':

$$Q(x, 17\ \text{Gen}\ r) \rightarrow Bew_c\left[Sb\left(r\,{}^{17}_{Z(x)}\right)\right]$$

$$Q(x, 17\ \text{Gen}\ r) \rightarrow Bew_c\left[Neg\ Sb\left(r\,{}^{17}_{Z(x)}\right)\right]$$

Instead of simply viewing the statements as metalogical propositions about the provability of arithmetical-foundational propositions, we can instead see the *meta-metalogical* relation holding between the two 'terms', "$Q(x$, 17 Gen $r)$" and

"$Bew_c\left[Sb\left(r\,{}^{17}_{Z(x)}\right)\right]$",

say $QR(Bew)$. One might as well then question the recursive enumerability of said 'meta-metalogical' propositions, inquiring whether or not said language will not fall prey to the very same specter of undecidability. This is indeed a perspicacious question, but it is in fact not one which is absolutely necessary to answer, in order to determine the consistency and completeness of the metalanguage that is reality. As we mentioned previously, the structure of the

CTMU—and consequently that of ultimate reality—is constructed via a novel form of *induction*. Given the facts of *perception* and *existence*, coupled with the fact that said perceptions are 'in motion', continuously evolving and maintaining logical stability (non-contradiction), we can determine *by neccessity* that the identity of reality (see the principle of syndiffeonesis) must be a *consistent* system, in terms of its extension and a *complete* system in terms of its intension.

From the *principle of explosion*, whereby any statement can be proved from a contradiction, we know that it must be the case that there are no contradictions within the metalanguage of reality, as if there were, nothing could be successfully distinguished from its logical complement. Additionally, from reality's self-referential nature (see the principle of syndiffeonesis and the property of self-dual self- containment), we can see that reality must possess a sort of 'self-checking' mechanism, such that *derivability*—via self-modeling in the model-theoretic sense—is in lockstep with *provability*.

2.72 For the Gödelian statements

$$Q(x, 17\ \mathrm{Gen}\ r) \rightarrow Bew_c\left[Sb\left(r\ {}^{17}_{Z(x)}\right)\right]$$

$$Q(x, 17\ \mathrm{Gen}\ r) \rightarrow Bew_c\left[Neg\ Sb\left(r\ {}^{17}_{Z(x)}\right)\right]$$

integrating these into a previously mentioned 'meta-metalogical' system can be done in a relatively straightforward manner—by molding both perceptual and cognitive syntax (rules of operation) to accompany such statements. Starting from the principle of syndiffeonesis and the givens of perception and existence, and adding the corollary that all that is real can be linguistically referenced and possesses a consistent and complete logical undergirding, we come to the (necessary) conclusion that perception and cognition abide by linguistically referenceable, logical rules or *syntax*. Langan, in his *The Cognitive-Theoretic Model of the Universe: A New Kind of Reality Theory* (2002), partitions the syntax of the mind into the following dynamically interdependent categories—space-time-object syntax, logico-mathematical syntax, qualio- perceptual syntax, and emo-telic syntax. In this instance with Gödel, we will call a 'meta-metalogical' symbol (including brackets/parentheses) $\varkappa x$ with the x taking either a 'world' class such that $\varkappa W$, a 'perception' class such that $\varkappa P$ in addition to a 'cognition' class, such that $\varkappa C$. For each and every symbol of the two previously mentioned Gödelian statements, we assign a corresponding $\varkappa W$ and, then, for simplicity's sake, we assign each term τW of the given statement corresponding terms of perception and cognition, τP and τC. We would then have the following 'templates' for each of the Gödelian statements:

Metalogical statement X (Gödel):

$$Q(x, 17 \text{ Gen } r) \rightarrow Bew_c\left[Sb\left(r\, {}^{17}_{Z(x)}\right)\right]$$

Meta-metalogical statement X (Langan):

$$\forall \kappa_{Wx} \exists \kappa_{Px} \exists \kappa_{Cx} [(\kappa_{Wx} \in \mathcal{K} \wedge (\kappa_{Wx} \rightarrow \kappa_{Px}) \wedge (\kappa_{Wx} \rightarrow \kappa_{Cx})],$$

where $(\kappa_{W1}, \kappa_{W2}, \ldots, \kappa_{W17}) \subseteq \mathcal{K}_W$

Metalogical statement Y (Gödel):

$$Q(x, 17 \text{ Gen } r) \rightarrow Bew_c\left[Neg\ Sb\left(r\, {}^{17}_{Z(x)}\right)\right]$$

Meta-metalogical statement Y (Langan):

$$\forall \kappa_{Wx} \exists \kappa_{Px} \exists \kappa_{Cx} [(\kappa_{Wx} \in \mathcal{K} \wedge (\kappa_{Wx} \rightarrow \kappa_{Px}) \wedge (\kappa_{Wx} \rightarrow \kappa_{Cx})],$$

where $(\kappa_{W1}, \kappa_{W2}, \ldots, \kappa_{W18}) \subseteq \mathcal{K}_W$

2.73 Wittgenstein's "notorious paragraph" then can be seen as an insightful yet somewhat imprecise recognition of the existence of 'nested' or *stratified* truth, of which Tarski's hierarchy of languages provides a perfect example. Tarski, addressing various paradoxes of self- referntiality, delineates a hierarchy of languages starting with an interpreted language $\mathcal{L}_0$ with *no* truth predicate, moving on to $\mathcal{L}_1$ which contains a truth predicate, such that this predicate only applies to sentences of $\mathcal{L}_0$. And then, if we wish to find truth in $\mathcal{L}_1$, we must move up to $\mathcal{L}_2$, which contains a truth predicate that only applies to sentences of $\mathcal{L}_1$, and so on *ad universae identitatem.* Wittgenstein, in pointing out the logical peculiarity inherent within the rapid-fire veridical alternation employed by Gödel in his incompleteness proof— though, to be sure, not disputing the result, but rather questioning its implications—unwittingly points to Tarski's hierarchy and its omnipresence, even in matters of formal undecidability. As Wittgenstein contends, the sentence '(17 Gen *r*) is not provable in Russell's system', if taken to be false, equates to 'false in Russell's system' which then entails 'it is provable that Neg [(17 Gen *r*) is not provable in Russell's system]', thus entailing that we must "give up" the purported unprovability. Additionally, if we take '(17 Gen *r*) is not provable in Russell's system' to be *true* where this equates to 'true in Russell's system', we must as well give up the purported unprovability. To be sure, Gödel did certainly prove that such an arithmetical system as Principia Mathematica is incomplete, but, resolutely, *he did not prove that the hierarchy of metalanguages above is incomplete.*

2.74 In Torkel Franzen's addmitedly eloquently written and insightful *Gödel's Theorem: An Incomplete Guide to its Use and Abuse* (2005) we see an improper declaration to the effect that mathematical truth can be pragmatically *separated* from metaphysical truth and reference—"It was emphasized that the mere fact of a consistent system *S* proving, for example, that there are infinitely many twin primes by no means implies that the twin prime hypothesis is true. Here again it is often thought that such an observation involves dubious metaphysical ideas. But no metaphysics is involved, only ordinary mathematics…'Every theorem of [Peano Arithmetic] is true' is a mathematical statement, not a statement about what can be proved or seen to be true, or a philosophical statement about mathematical reality." This dismissal of the intersection of metaphysical and logical truth is redolent of Rorty's dismissal of Truth (and indeed *t*ruth as well) on the grounds that the mind is no "mirror of nature"; it is a willful disengagement from logical reasoning under the *premise* that said reasoning cannot provide us with a sturdy metaphysical foundation. In the same vein, Franzén artificially separates metaphysics from mathematical truth, under the *premise* that metaphysical truth is of a categorically different kind than that of mathematics. We can see from the CTMU that, due to the principle of syndiffeonesis—ultimately resulting in conspansion and the self-generative nature of reality—logical truth is in fact within the 'domain' of metaphysical truth or, more precisely, logical truth ranges over the *theory* (in the model-theoretic sense) of reality.

2.75 For Gödel's subsequent disjunction, "The Mathematics either is too big for the human brain or the man's mind is something besides a simple machine", it is the case that the latter portion is true, while the former false.

2.8 Definitively, from the CTMU, we have attained the conceptual machinery of Leibniz's famed calculus ratiocinator. And, indeed, Frege was quite right to view his logic as a *universal* language of concepts; predicate logic is everywhere needed to maintain the intelligibility of not only mere concepts but of reality itself as well.

2.9 Given that reality is not static but rather is continuously evolving, we require a reality-theoretic notion with which to 'chart' this ontological motion. In turn, given that reality is everywhere linguistically referenceable and logically buttressed, and given that *information* is at its core a construct binary in nature, undergirded by two- valued logic, information becomes a crucial point of reality-theoretic analysis

2.91 As the field of cybernetics has not been erected upon reality-theoretic grounds, it is thus unsuitable for our purposes. But we may certainly 'retool' it, incorporating predicate logic, model theory and language theory (generative grammar), in order to align its expressive capacity with the nature of reality.

2.92 In a cybernetic arrangement with a *sensor*, a *controller* and an external 'system' that is acted upon, we have an arrangement in which there are objects posed in an unreferenced medium. As a consequence of this, we cannot use such an arrangement as the basis of reality theory.

2.93 Where all the contents or 'sets' of reality double as descriptively-implicating vessels of syntax and information, we must allow information to flow through all things real, setting no artificial boundaries. We may call this novel form of information theory *metacybernetics.*

2.94 This metacybernetics, as Langan has conceived of it, is of a fundamentally different kind than is "second-order cybernetics". Second-order cybernetics simply places the mind in a dual role as sensor *and* controller, while maintaining a segmented, linearly-bound metaphysics.

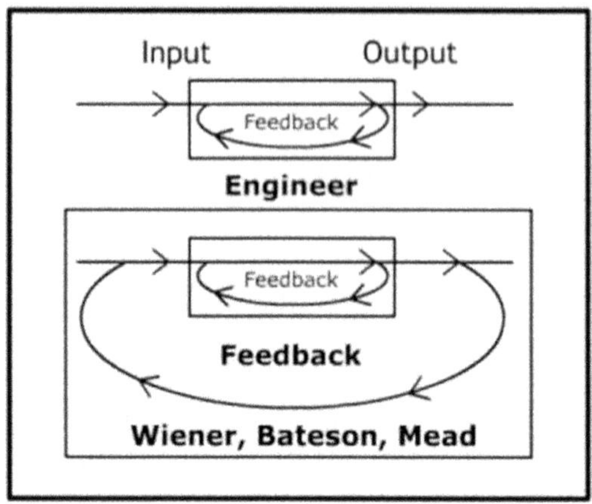

For if we merely fit the mind into the sensor-controller dichotomy, while leaving syntax (the rules of the system) vaguely 'out there', still residing in the minds of the very observers *performing* said "second-order cybernetics", we are still neglecting to include a core component of reality into the cybernetic system, *theorization itself*; universe of discourse is cleaved from theory.

3 In again considering *conspansion*, the process through which the universe continuously rescales itself (keeping invariant), and combining this fact with the descriptive containment of the 'complementive' syntax of reality within each real object, we can gain great insight on the nature of the evolution of reality. In placing the *endomorphism* that results from descriptive containment side-by-side with the *ectomorphic* transitioning of objects topologically contained by reality through space, we reach a new duality principle—*conspansive duality*. Due to the principle of syndiffeonesis, we see that the universe cannot, *a priori*, evolve ectomorphically. But we also see that objects do indeed, from our perception, transition through time ectomorphically. So how are these two seemingly contradicting views reconciled in the CTMU? In the CTMU, there are *two phases* of conspansion, *inner expansion* and *collapse*; the former

corresponding to the time evolution of the wave function and the latter corresponding to the collapse of the wavefunction.

3.1 By the principle of syndiffeonesis, *the laws of physics* cannot exist outside of reality. The laws of physics must then derive from the identity of reality, what Langan terms M, symbolic for 'metaformal system'. But we seem to have a problem: examining the two phases of conspansion, inner expansion and collapse, we see no viable portion into which the generation of physical law could fit, as both phases seem to require such laws to already be in place; in inner expansion we require laws of electromagnetism and gravitation and in collapse we of course require/implicate these forces and more. We now of course have the resulting question: what is the *mechanism* via which laws of physics are generated and *of what* are these laws *made*?

3.11 We can see that laws are not logically self-sufficient. That is, the laws of physics can only be defined with respect to the objects and attributes upon which they act. And, even more, both objects and attributes themselves, in order to transition in state (temporally), must be implicated by said laws. We can view this dynamic symbolically where all temporal transitions of objects $O_x \rightarrow O_x$ are necessarily of the form $L(O)$: $L_x(A_x O_x) \rightarrow A_y(O_x)$ and also where L takes no other parameters other than attributes and objects. We may be tempted to explain this mutual dependency by invoking the identity of reality, M, stating that M is the 'law of all laws' but this would violate the principle of syndiffeonesis, as which law would dictate that M were to be said 'law of all laws'?; we would be locked into an infinite nomological regress. In order that we escape this regress, then, there must be a fundamental something which is neither a law nor an object/attribute, something that both (a) requires no external explanation and (b) gives rise to both nomological strings and objects and attributes upon which said strings act. This fundamental something must be a sort of *infocognitive potential*, in that it gives rise to both object and syntax, where the former roughly corresponds to *information* and the latter to *cognition.* Langan terms this infocognitive potential *telesis.*

3.12 Examining the notion of 'potential' we can refer to the notions of inner expansion and collapse for heuristic purposes. In Langan's paper "The Metaformal System: Completing the Theory of Language" (2018) he refers to inner expansion as a *distributive ectomorphism*, a one-to- many mapping which outwardly distributes compact *identities* (states, points) to *potentials*, and he refers to collapse as a *distributive endomorphism*, a one-to-many dual mapping which inwardly distributes *attributes* to *states* or points. Where said 'potentials' are seen as possible points/locations of eventual collapse and where laws are seen as rules by which said potentials will abide, once 'actualized', it is apparent that (potentials + laws = states), but, at the same time, it is not apparent how laws are formed 'in between' both the *d-ectomorphism* and the *d-endomorphism* and the former's mapping of state to potential and the latter's mapping of attribute to state.

3.121 It is apparent that—as the process of conspansion is necessarily atemporal—both d-ectomorphism and d-ectomorphism *cannot be timelike*, that is they must run *orthogonal* to the state transitions we observe in the universe.

3.122 We can make the necessity of orthogonality more apparent by meditating on the nature of the *identity* of reality. It has been mentioned that the stability of perception necessitates that the system of reality be both consistent and complete; in fact, reality must be consistent and complete with respect to definitive, descriptive and interpretative dimension. Where state transition is seen as a nomological-temporal dynamic and, again, where said state transition can be considered *continuous*, that is without discrete 'jumping' in and out of existence, the process that generates laws must run alongside the temporal domain, so to speak.

3.13 The orthogonal relationship of the conspansive semimodel to the linear progression of objects through time is redolent of the relationship between the nonterminal portion of a syntax tree and its terminal portion. In this case, the terminal portion can be viewed as collections of states, whereas the nonterminal portion can be seen as a grouping of various syntax components utilized by reality in the production of the terminal states. Langan groups both the d-ectomorphism and the d-endomorphism under the non-terminal 'semilanguage' Ls, while terming the linear terminal semilanguage Lo. This means that, when considering the form of a syntax tree, for each terminal expression, there exists a statement of Ls as an *internal node* of the tree. According to this, then, laws of physics exist as an internal node, above any given terminal output. *Prior* to (in the nonterminal sense) both the d- ectomorphism, the mapping of state to potential, and the d-endomorphism, the mapping of attribute (adjusted scale) to state, a *nomological string* must exist, dictating the particular manner of which the morphisms will be carried out.

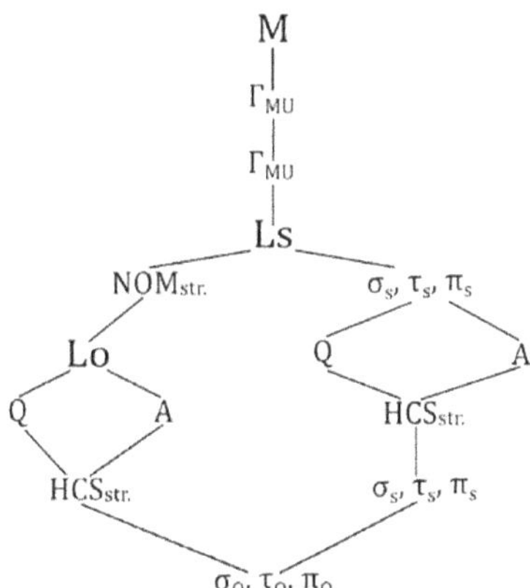

This isn't to say, however, that there is no *invariance* when it comes to conspansion; the rate of inner expansion is invariant and the rate of 'shrinkage' or rescaling is time-independent.

3.131 The rate of inner expansion must be constant, as, if it were not, the principle of syndiffeonesis would be violated. Imagine two objects, x and y, at a metaphorical 'starting line' in space, both perfectly aligned by some distance metric. Suppose that, at the 'firing of the gun', object x raced out of the blocks, leaving y in the dust, where in terms of speed (ignoring acceleration) $x >_V y$. Let's say that the distance from the starting line to the 'boundary' of the universe is d. It is easy to see that if the speed of x is sufficiently fast and the distance d is sufficiently small, x will exceed the bounds of the universe and, we have seen, by the principle of syndiffeonesis, that something cannot exceed the bounds of the universe, as it would still be, strictly speaking, *within the universe*! Further then, in this case, the crux of the issue is that, in order for reality to determine whether x or y is traveling at a faster rate, is to 'observe' it *transition in state.* That is, reality cannot skirt around the issue by simply proactively monitoring the speed of all its contents, so as to prevent violation of the principle of syndiffeonesis, as, even if it were to have such an ability, it would still be left vulnerable to such a scenario (and others of the same form): say $x >_V y$ and the distance from the 'starting line' to the 'boundary' of the universe is d; suppose that, for the universe to check the velocity of x it must observe it transition in state for t_P, a unit of Planck time and, then, also suppose that $d = \ell_P$, the Planck length, and that the velocity of x is such that $x >_V t_P$.

3.132 The rate of requantization (rescaling) must *a priori* be atemporal or, perhaps more precisely, *metatemporal.* Let's say that reality requantized its universe 'internally', that is, from a sort of 'control center' topologically contained within itself. The first hurdle to cross would be the mighty feat of a temporally-bound object 'reaching' outside of time to manipulate its set-theoretic complement. And, even if, paradoxically, this hurdle were cleared, then this control center would have to requantize *itself.* But, if said control center were to requantize itself, it would necessarily do so *through time.* Even if the time taken for the control center to requantize itself were the Planck time t_P, the logical reverberations from such a scale discontinuity would impale the heart of reality, so to speak. Conclusively, if it were not metatemporal, there would be discontinuity of scale. For much the same reasons, spacetime itself must be requantized, as opposed to merely the objects 'within'. Reality itself is its own model, serving as both theory and universe of discourse. Not only this, but, given the dynamic nature of reality, it must serve as a constantly evolving, dually informing theory-universe coupling. With each self-interpretation-in the broadest sense-syntax becomes state. And, with each self-refinement of theory, state becomes syntax. It may at first seem counterintuitive that with the ostensibly *solely syntactic* refinement of reality's theory (set of axioms) that state becomes syntax. But this is true by virtue of the metatemporal, generative nature of reality. For reality's theory to be self-refined, reality must 'sample' the given mass-energy distribution of the universe, so as to ensure complete and accurate nomological application. Additionally, as observers (us humans, etc.) are both members of reality's universe of discourse and ingredients of the syntax of reality (its theory), various observed states are integrated into the syntax of reality, from universe to theory.

3.2 We stated before: *prior* to both the d-ectomorphism, the mapping of state to potential, and the d- endomorphism, the mapping of attribute (adjusted scale) to state, a *nomological string* must exist, dictating the particular manner of which the morphisms will be carried out. What we meant by this is that for both a [(*state*) → (*potential*)] and a [(*attributes*) → (*state*)] form, we need nomological strings to determine in what manner the consequent term will be 'informed by' the antecedent term *and vice versa.* For instance, where 'state' is considered as the position and velocity of a given particle or collection thereof, and where a potential is a possible state, considering the application of a nomological string, the substituted state in the [(state) → (*potential*)] form will necessarily abide by the laws which dictated the potential, just as the potential necessarily abided by the *previous* state.

3.21 As an illustration of what we mean by "prior", we can show a rough outline of a generative syntax tree roughly corresponding to the dynamic of reality.

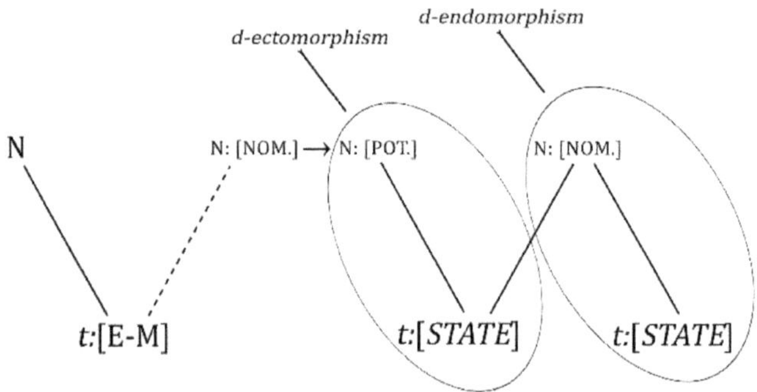

N here represents a non-terminal expression and *t* a terminal one, while E-M is the energy-mass distribution of the universe. Seeing the categorization of both {N: [POT.] → *t*:[STATE]} and {N: [NOM.] → *t*:[STATE]}, one may very well question why we have neglected to categorize the {*t*: [E-M] | N: [NOM.]} dynamic seen on the left half of the above image. In fact, Langan gives this dynamic a specific name— *primary telic recursion.*

3.22 Observers are of course nested within this aforementioned primary telic recursion; they and the objects 'around' them are subject to both the nomological strings generated by the identity of reality and the higher-order syntax comprising it. But, it is also the case that observers draw upon telesis in their own manner, dynamically generating within the environment provided by what Langan sometimes terms the Primary telor.

One may object to our declaration that observers are free to generate relationships of syntax-state. This may be because there seems to be nothing analytic in the concept of self-causality which entails freedom of the will. This much may indeed be true, however, this fact does not impair the existence freewill whatsoever. To see more clearly the neccessity that is free will we should again mention the logical primacy of potential over both law and parameter. It may, prima facie, seem intuitive that a simple regress of law ($L_1 \rightarrow L_2, \ldots, L_{\infty+}$) should eventually lead to the identity of reality itself, such that this identity is the 'law of all laws', the prime nomological mover, so to speak. But we must remember that the relationship between laws and their parameters is a bijective one; we have the somewhat naive 'rule':

$$(L_x \equiv o_x) \wedge \neg\Diamond\, (\exists\, L_x \neg \exists\, o_x\, (L_x R o_x)).$$

We also of course have the following:

$$[(xRy \equiv x \cup\!\cap y) \wedge (L_x \equiv o_x)].$$

But then, where we view every unisection, $x \cup\!\cap y$ as one between parameters x_p and y_p, and a unifying law, $\cup\!\cap_L$,such that $x_p \cup\!\cap_L y_p$, we are faced with the regress ($x_p \cup\!\cap_L y_p, \ldots, M_p \cup\!\cap_L M_p$) all the way up to where the identity of reality itself serves as its own parameter. So then, if this basic (parameter-law-parameter) form holds all the way up to the very identity of reality, what is the nature of this bijection? We require a certain something, a certain third 'element' which is pre- parametric and pre-nomological in nature, something that can give rise to both laws and their parameters. This certain something must, in essence, 'blanket over' the entirety of reality, serving as both a rich logico- potential backdrop and an idempotency-sustaining ambience, allowing reality to enforce its consistency and completeness. Once we realize that even higher-order syntactic strings of reality are such 'laws' that we have been discussing, as they act upon other strings, serving as *parameters*, we determine that this something must be some sort of *potential*, as opposed to a syntactic string.

3.32 Where there is neither an infinite nomological regress, ($L_1 \rightarrow L_2, \ldots, L_{\infty+}$), nor a 'prime nomological mover', such that ($L_1 \rightarrow L_2, \ldots, M$), coupled with the fact that there is neither an infinite parametric regress nor a 'prime parametric mover', *there can be no determinism.*

3.321 Determinism is based upon the notion that between every nomological-parametric state transition, there is not only a cause but an externally determined one at that. As we have stated, Langan mentions the distinction between endomorphism and ectomorphism, where the former refers to something being mapped *inside of itself*, while the latter refers to something being mapped *outside of itself*. Due to the principle of syndiffeonesis and the subsequent neccessity of conspansion, the ectomorphism of linear state transition (objects 'through' space) is an ectomorphism merely by the embedment in the endomorphic conspansive "semimodel". Now, if one were to object that nothing *a priori* dictates that an endomorphic dynamic provide for the free will of its inhabitants, he would be missing one crucial point—where law and parameter continuously arise from a mutually primordial potential, there can be no string of ectomorphically or endomorphically determined causality.

4 St. Anselm of Canterbury's ontological argument for the existence of God is quite correct. However, those who have examined it for flaws and merits have so far failed to grasp its essence. The crux of the argument deals with three main concepts—*intension*, *extension* and *syntax*. Kant attributed the argument's ostensible failing to an improper use of existence, that is, treating existence as a predicate and expecting the result of the said Ex to fundamentally differ from the simple Ux or the x in the understanding. Alvin Plantinga in his brilliant *God*

and Other Minds (1967) correctly pointed out that Kant's criticism is not applicable, but he neglected to reach the core of the matter. Say that we consider St. Anselm's U*x* as $S_E(G_I)$ and his E*x* as $S_I(G_I)$, where S is the syntax of the human mind in question, G is the *intension* that is God, the subscripted E signifies that the mind in question takes G as an *extension* of his mind, while the subscripted I signifies that he takes G as an *intension* within his mind (and *outside* it as well). Whatever is an extension is in turn an intension for additional extensions, *as well as the converse.* (excluding of course limiting cases). But, in this example, where the intension that is God is seen as an extension of mental syntax S_E, there is of course no violation in accommodating for within S the requisites to see G as an intension, S_I, and *vice versa.* We then have the following *sound* statement:

$$(S_E \leftrightarrow S_I) \Rightarrow S_I(G_I).$$

4.1 Then, a simple CTMU-informed reading of the statement '$(S_E \leftrightarrow S_I) \Rightarrow S_I(G_I)$' shows that it is the case by virtue of reality's syntactic coherency and subsequent *intelligibility*. The fact that a contradiction results from $(S_E(G_I) \wedge \neg(S_I(G_I)))$ is because the *intension* of God in fact *distributes* over the statement, while, simultaneously, both statements are themselves members of the *extension* of God, such that we cannot assert $(S_E(G_I) \wedge \neg(S_I(G_I)))$ because reality is such that $([S_E(G_I), \neg(S_I(G_I))] \in G_I, G_E)$. If it were the case that $(S_E(G_I) \wedge \neg(S_I(G_I)))$ were contradiction free, then this would entail that something in the syntax of the mind S would prevent the mind from taking the form resulting in S_I. This, in turn, would entail that the intension of God would be *unintelligible.* And, if the intension of God were unintelligible then He would not have the capacity to sustain reality, as he must according to his very intension.

4.2 Regardless of whether or not Gödel's ontological proof stands firmly upon its own foundations, we can certainly interpret it in accordance with the CTMU, perhaps partially 'explaining' why its conclusion follows from its axioms. The main takeaway from the argument, a sort of meta-statement on its structure, we can call P1: Logically analyzing an individual in a certain manner, in an 'essential manner', and factoring in that the individual possesses, in its essence, a property that exemplifies all of these essences, entails that this individual is seen to be necessarily existing. Then, analyzing our (extremely naïve) metalanguage,$\mathcal{M}$,we can present a few translations from Göd el's proof into $\mathcal{M}$, borrowing notation from Dana Sco-tt's modal logic-based version of the proof.

$$G(x) \equiv \text{STATE}(G)$$

$$ess.(G) \equiv \text{SYNTAX}_{ess.}(G)$$

$$\varphi(G) \equiv \text{SYNTAX}\varphi(G) \text{ V } \text{STATE}\varphi(G)$$

$$P(G) \equiv \text{SYNTAX}_{P}(G)$$

Then, we can render the 'meat' of the proof in our metalanguage:

$$\{\text{P}[\text{SYNTAX}_{ess.}(G) \supset \text{SYNTAX}_{P}(G)\text{: } \forall\ \text{SYNTAX}_{ess.(x)}(G) \Longrightarrow$$

$$\exists\ \text{SYNTAX}_{ess.(x)}(G)\} \Longrightarrow \Box\exists x G(x)$$

What we mean by this is that, given the totality of syntax of God, when it has a subset 'positive property', $\text{SYNTAX}_{P}(G)$, such that this subset, for all essences of God (equivalent to the totality of His syntax), 'exemplifies' each of these essences, such that $\exists\ \text{SYNTAX}_{ess.(x)}(G)$, then this entails that $\Box\exists x$ ($\text{STATE}_{x}(G)$ A P[$\text{SYNTAX}_{ess.(x)}(G)$]). What we have here is a case of *self-reference*, via a mediating syntax. The basic form at work: $\text{SYNTAX}_{ess.}(G)\{\text{SYNTAX}_{P}(G_{)*as\ rule\ of\ syntax*} \rightarrow \text{SYNTAX}_{ess.}(G)\}$. In other words, the positive property of 'necessary existence' is a string that acts upon itself, through a cooperating syntax. Now, in the CTMU, that a syntax can *act upon itself* does indeed imply that it exists 'external' to the mind, that is it is not possible that it is a mere whimsical fantasy. Take for example tertiary syntactors, mere particles. These entities cannot self-model, requiring the aid of secondary telors or the Primary telor (God Himself). Just as well, take for example a memory or a certain other 'qualia' of the mind. These entities presuppose and require the mind itself for any sort of self-reference; the mind here can be seen to play the mediating syntax. Here we have a prime example of the difference between the contemporary distinction between syntax and semantics and the Langanian distinction between syntax and *state*. Within the language of the higher-order modal logic used by Dana Scott in his rendition of the proof, we of course can see the syntax-semantics distinction. But, in our metalanguage $\mathcal{M}$, we can make the higher-level distinction of syntax-state even between terms including both syntax and semantics. Here we have just given an *ontological* reason or 'grounding' for why the inference within the object-level modal logic stands as it does.

5 Although Langan's CTMU represents a reality theory in which both the informational and mental aspects are equally as real, it would be rather incorrect to state that, in the CTMU, the mind *supervenes upon* information. In contemporary philosophy of mind, it is often seen as indubitably self-evident that mental processes supervene upon physical ones; this is the axiom upon which the entire edifice is built. But, in taking such an axiom, one is presupposing the ostensible *separation* between the mental and the informational. Where Langan has constructed the CTMU via a novel form of reasoning—reasoning by *inducto-neccessity*—to attempt to parse, or supplement it with simple axiomatic constructions is doomed to fail. By (i) the principle of syndiffeonesis, (ii) the subsequent neccessity of conspansion, (iii) the linguistic nature of

perception, cognition and thus reality as a whole and (iv) the neccessity that information be self-processed (by reality itself), Langan determines that mind, instead of resting in a mere relationship of supervenience upon information, is instead intrinsically coupled with said information, comprising the monic 'substance' that he terms *infocogntion.*

5.1 From *constructive-filtrative duality* and the *metatemporal* nature of the syntax of Ls, we find that the mathematical structure known as the *lattice* can be particularly useful in displaying infocognitive dynamics and operations. Lattice theory, at its core, is intimately coupled with partially- ordered sets or *posets*; a partial order is any binary relation that is *reflexive* (each element is comparable to itself), *antisymmetric* (no two different elements precede each other), and *transitive* (the start of a chain of precedence relations must precede the end of the chain). Hasse diagrams, so- called "transitive reductions" of the given poset they represent, are in many cases lattices. But of course not all lattices are also Hasse diagrams. Lattices, on the other hand, have the capacity to be extremely *general*, certainly a boon in terms of mathematical structures. In fact, we can arrange a lattice oriented along two axes, one temporal and one spatial, such that both events and/or particles and minds are represented in dynamic contact and relationship. We should mention, however, that the structure we present does *not* in fact conform to the mathematical definition of a lattice, rather, it can simply be termed an *ordering*. The reason for this is that, in terms of spatio-temporally extended contact, there are numerous syndiffeonic 'paths' for each sever, as opposed to there being a unique *GLB* and *LUB* for each.

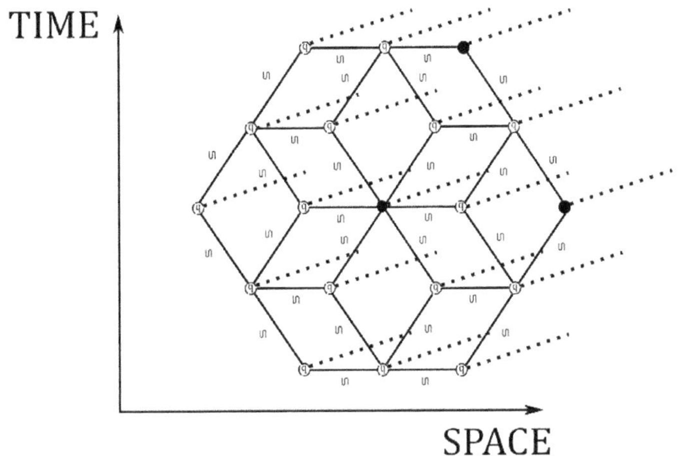

Here 'q' represents a general event or collection of particles, while the black circles represent observers; the dotted lines represent the extension of the simple 2D (plus time) diagram to incorporate 3D (plus time) dynamics. And, of course, for events clustering together in either (or both) space and time, the 'resolution' of the lattice can increase in tandem. To better imagine such an increase of resolution, one can simply notice the hexagonal self-similarity of the lattice above; the portion displayed is itself hexagonal, while its 2D 'contents' consist of six hexagonal structures, of which partially overlap. To increase the resolution of the lattice, all one would need to do then would be to recursively replicate the structure of the contents of the main hexagonal structure within the smaller hexagonal structures. The set of all circles which a given observer is in contact with (observationally interacting with) in any given time slice can be seen as a sort of 'current world' set, all that exists to the mind in question at a certain moment. Following this, all circles that are connected to a given observer's 'current world' are possible ingredients of metatemporal interaction. One, at first, may wonder why the structure of the lattice is necessary, that is, why there must be spacelike, polyhedral connections (though the exact 'shape' of the connections is rather arbitrary) between events and observers. In asking this, the inquirer is likely clinging to the *linear-evolutive* picture of reality. Due to the nature of reality, events are in contact with one another *metatemporally*.

5.11 Utilizing the infocognitive lattice diagram we have just created, we will illustrate the differences between inner expansion (local) and coinversion (global) and requantization (local) and incoversion (global).

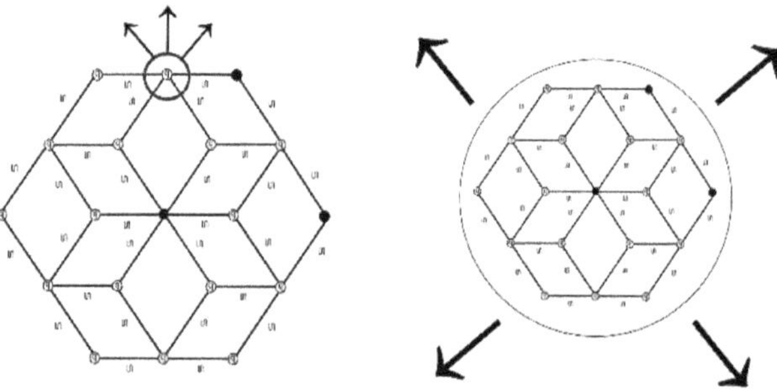

Pondering on the nature of requantization, we eventually come to the conclusion that both its local and global components must occur *metasimultaneously*, as, if they did not, discontinuity of scale would implode the consistency (self-recognition) of the universe. *As man gazes at God's creation, God in turn gazes at man.*

5.2 The sheer profundity of metatemporal interaction can be evinced simply by considering the ever-present adjacency of *paradox* at each turn, for the Primary telor or *God.* The entire collection of events within the universe, past and future, is in fact *metadetermined.* Yet, given the generative freedom of God and His higher- order vantage point of linear, time-dependent reality, a metadetermined reality is in no way a deterministic reality. Indeed, God has the capacity to revise and alter portions of time-dependent reality, *acting across the temporal axis, as if it were a spatial one.* Here we can ascertain that there are two main varieties of evolution—*temporally-bound* evolution and *metatemporal* evolution. God, in the conduction of his metatemporal evolution of reality, must be precise enough to immunize the temporally-bound events themselves against paradox; scaling, spatial dynamics, nomological dependencies, and temporal invariants must remain seamlessly intermeshed, throughout the process of metatemporal evolution. And, given the principle of syndiffeonesis, the neccessity of tautological 'embedment' and the subsequent *logico-linguistic* nature of reality, we can combine (a) the fact that perception and existence are stable (moment-by-moment) and (b) that reality is system abiding by, and generating, certain logically-buttressed rules, we can conclude that God must in fact evolve *seamlessly*—without logical inconsistency—in his metatemporal manner.

5.3 The illustrious problem of evil can be represented as the following chain of reasoning:

(i) $(\exists\ G \supset (Omp(G),\ Onm(G),\ M(G))$ | $G =_{def}$ God; $Omp =_{def}$ omnipotent; $Onm =_{def}$ omniscient; $M =_{def}$ morally perfect

(ii) $Omp(G) \supset \Diamond[\forall\ x \neg\ (evil(x))]$

(iii) $Onm(G) \supset G\text{: } K(\forall\ x\ [(evil(x)) \vee \neg\ (evil(x))])$ | $K =_{def}$ epistemic operator

(iv) $M(G) \supset G\text{: } D(\forall\ x\ (evil(x))\ [f\ (evil(x))\text{: } \{(evil(x)) \rightarrow \neg\ (evil(x))\}])$ | $D =_{def}$ operator of desire; $f =_{def}$ generic function

(v) $\exists\ x\ (evil(x))$

(vi) $(\exists\ x\ (evil(x)) \wedge \exists\ G) \supset G\text{: } \neg\ (Omp(G) \wedge Onm(G) \wedge M(G))$

(vii) $\neg \exists\ G$

The 'link' in the chain that is the weakest—(ii). In terms of (i), we will take no major issue, as it is not rigorously defined what exactly is meant by omnipotence, omniscience and moral perfection; additionally, it is intuitive enough that the Supreme Being should indeed exhibit all such properties, when they are construed as limiting aspects of reality. We should now address a few background assumptions lurking beneath statement (ii).

For one, that omnipotence should entail the ability to effectively hamper each and every *freely chosen* act which happens to be evil is rather hastily assumed. Without giving due consideration to the overall *structure* of reality (or God), it is assumed that God's power scales isomorphically with the capacity to intervene with and limit the freedom of His inhabitants. Given that (ii) sidesteps the issue of determining the structure of reality and God—while additionally assuming that said structure has no impact upon the ostensibly intimate connection between omnipotence and the eradication of evil—we can decidedly omit it from any further consideration, thus contingently collapsing the above chain of reasoning.

5.31 One could attempt to claim that the Primary telor, God—being in total control of the formation of nomological strings could simply alter the laws of physics, so as to prevent the generation of evil. This is an intuitively pleasing suggestion, but it carries no weight within the supertautology that is the CTMU. To see why, we need only consider the nature of telic recursion, the process by which observers or secondary telors channel the primordial stuff' (potential) of reality. Each instance of telic recursion is an instance of generation *ab potentia*, the CTMU-informed counterpart of the generation *ab nihilo*. That is, between every given desire, d and action a, there is a generation from UBT (unbound telesis), $d \leadsto_{\text{UBT}} a$. And, in terms of God, He must generate nomological strings from UBT, just as observers refine their syntax-state relationships from UBT as well. Let's say that within a change of time between ($\sim_{UBT}$) and (*a*), Δt, God arranges the laws of physics such that only the smallest bundle of particles within the brain permitting sensing/action can interact, such that only a binary is permitted, $a_x \vee \neg a_x$. Focusing then on the conventio-social aspect of the situation, it is inevitable that norms and conventions would be erected around such a dichotomy $a_x \vee \neg a_x$. And, adding in feelings and desires, such that these are not freely generated, a system of expression centered on the combinations of actions and desire could be roughly fleshed out. Subsequently, given that adherence to/alteration of what Langan terms the generalized utility of reality is ultimately a process of sensing (or feeling) and acting, even from such a limited choice of actions, $ax \vee \neg ax$, *deviance from generalized utility could arise.*

5.312 Revisiting statement (ii) from above, '$Omp(G) \supset \Diamond[\forall x \neg (evil(x))]$' we see that we must either adjust the notion of omnipotence accordingly or do away with it in its entirety. But, in examining the structure and subsequent genesis of reality, we see that to perform the latter task would be ill-guided. Drawing from a contemporary analysis of the topic, that presented by Thomas P. Flint and Alfred J. Freddoso in their "Maximal Power" (1983), we will state that actions of observers cannot be *strongly actualized*; "Roughly, an agent *S* strongly actualizes a state of affairs *p* just when *S* causally determines *p*'s obtaining, i.e., just when *S* does something which in conjunction with other operative causal factors constitutes a sufficient causal condition for *p*'s obtaining." We make a much stronger claim than this, however; we can show the precise ontologico-structural underpinnings of and reasons for this fact.

5.313 As opposed to the verbose definition of omnipotence

—"S is omnipotent at t in W if and only if for any state of affairs p and…"

—provided by Flint and Freddoso, the CTMU-informed definition of omnipotence considers a few single aspects of reality's intrinsic form and all- embracing ontological structure and potential. For all real things syntactically mapped to from God Himself, can we not say that that which affords them their very existence (God of course), possesses maximal *ontologico-generative* power? More specifically, the structure of reality permitting the very generation of real things from UBT is such that its contents continue to exist *iff* it continues to differentiate itself from that which it is not, tautological 'root'. Should not this ontological biconditional, combined with the ontologico-generative primacy of its consequent, entail the omnipotence of God, despite His inability to prevent evil actions? What should take primacy here is that *God can indeed prevent evil actions*, by ceasing to provide the ontological potential for their very existence (and, by implication of course the very observers that generate such evil). What we can say definitively—observers can be seen as *extensions of the structure of God*, indeed *parts* of Him, such that the (lower-level) structure affording the coherence of these observers is—*while God continues to assert His identity*— immune to diversion and/or impedance of the dynamic capacity that is the *freedom of the will.*

5.4 As for the question of why observers or, as Langan has sometimes called them, 'sensor-controllers', exist in the first place or, more strongly, why they are *required* by the identity of reality, we may present a list of naïve propositions to illustrate several thought-provoking points and questions:

(i) If God Himself were to rescale and inner expand particles, what utility would there be to maximize? Presumably he might attempt to arrange particles in a 'pleasing manner'; but pleasing in what manner? Where aesthetic pleasure is derived from *unexpected*, novel interweaving, what could possibly be unexpected to God in a world of particles subject to divinely-generated nomological strings and topological interfacing?

(ii) If we are talking about particles only, as opposed to sensor-controllers, what means would God use to judge the arrangement pleasing?

a. If we say that He had syntactic requirements of aesthetic pleasure then this would raise the point of there being *no time-restrictions* or requirements upon such atemporal changes in syntax; why would God then need a time-dependent realm?

b. And, since particles have no 'senses' through which to inform God of utility, thus resulting in a sum total of generalized utility, we can say that syntax, in the case of an observerless universe, the only means through which God could judge utility.

(iii) Thus, eliminating the time-dependent, linear language of Lo entirely, it could be stated that God, without observers, would be in an intrinsically utility-free state.

(iv) From such a utility-free state, it *cannot* be said that God created (via *metaphysically*-guided evolution) sensor- controllers to 'increase' His utility, as before creation there could indeed be *no notion.*

(v) Given that God, without sensor-controllers, 'senses' no time, that is, His existence is *at all levels* (as the metaphysical level would be the *only* level) self- encased and *self-caused*, there could be no evolution, as both (a) He would intrinsically take the "MU form", the metaphysical form from which all physical arrangements can and *do* draw upon and (b) any ostensible 'addition' upon the MU form, without physical, temporally-bound output would be akin to God showing himself that which He *already knew*.

5.41 So then, if God were to have *any notion of utility*, what Langan terms *generalized utility*, He would require us sensor controllers, freely generating new syntax-state relationships and, in acting in accordance with their own lower-level utility functions, having an impact upon generalized utility, for better or for worse.

5.42 It cannot be that God generated sensor-controllers in order to gain or increase His lot; we are not ourselves experiments subject to the fickle whim of the Almighty. Rather, God can be seen to have *sacrificed* his perfect ontological stasis, in order to generate us. Before sensor-controllers there was neither 'positive' utility nor 'negative' utility; in creating the observer, in granting some of his subcomponents the freedom to generate syntax-state relationships, God opened Himself up to inevitable *deviation* from His intrinsic, ontologically supreme form, the MU form.

6 Previously, in showing an example of an infocognitive lattice, comprising black 'observer' circles • and white event/particle circles ◦, we may have given some a wrong intuition of how the evolution of reality works. Instead of the process being a static, receptive dynamic, in which observers have external events 'connected to' or impressed upon them, the evolution of reality occurs in a generative, 'active' manner. As we have established, the contents of the universe do *not* evolve in *only*

linear fashion; from the principle of syndiffeonesis, the subsequent neccessity of conspansion and the mutual dependency of nomological strings and their parameters—reality both (a) evolves in a non-linear manner (in conjunction with its terminal, linear 'output') and (b) the process through which state and syntax evolve is fundamentally a process from *potential*. What this means is that 'beneath' the motion of a celestial body around its star, 'behind' the 'jiggling' of cells throughout the body, there is a punctuated, non-linear process of generation from potential at work.

6.1 This aforementioned binding of ontological potential requires a very special configuration. That which can bind telesis must have a requisite organizational complexity; secondary telors possess the capacity to *model their cognitive processes*. Whereas for tertiary syntactors, the generation of nomological strings by the Primary telor (God)—excluding the perceptual events in which sensor-controllers implicate them in—is the primary means through which they evolve. For these particles (tertiary syntactors), the interpretation function assigning members of the universe of discourse to the symbols of its linear-governing language Lo, is provided by the Primary telor and the various secondary telors (sensor-controllers) implicated. On the other hand, for secondary telors, in addition to them 'receiving' various interpretations by the Primary telor, some of the interpretations of its higher-order language Ls are provided by themselves; in this sense sensor-controllers are considered to have the capacity to *self-model*. This dynamic of self-modeling should *not* be equated with reflection, introspection or metacognition, as none of these is strictly required in order that a telor provide an interpretation for a collection of symbols of its cognitive-perceptual syntax of Ls.

6.11 To state once more—the process through which secondary (and the Primary) telor(s) bind telesis and, metasimultaneously, self-model, is termed telic recursion. When engaging in telic recursion and consequently 'rising above' the terminal language of Lo, it can be loosely said that telors gain access to a 'higher' realm, a realm in which things are not ordered by time; *syntax* is the only 'glue' in the *metaphysical* language of Ls. When ascending *solely* to the level of Ls, secondary telors gain access to the atemporal, time-as-space nonterminal portion of reality. Whereas, in the linear- ectomorphic semimodel—the portion of reality in which evolution appears as linear change of state—one cannot step out from within the 'flow' of time, in Ls, secondary telors gain access to the *dual* representation of events as dynamically, metatemporally connected inner expansive domains. Whereas, in the l-ectomorphic semimodel, superposition is parametrized by time, in the conspansive semimodel, at the level of Ls, superposition is parametrized by *space.* The overlaying of inner expansive domains (regions of nomological distribution implicating previously (temporally) occurring events/interactions), takes the form of overlapping and intersecting 'venn diagrams', dualizing temporal *construction* into spatial *filtration.*

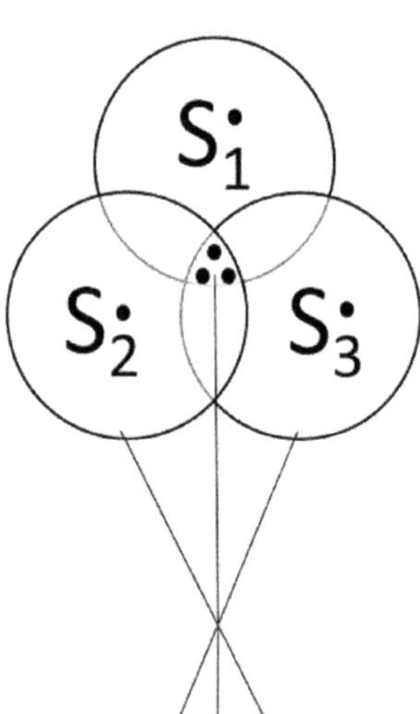

How do telors 'orient' themselves, in the process of making decisions via telic recursion? Well, via their structural complexity—in either both Ls and Lo or in Ls only—telors, according to their relevant constraints, choose a certain syntax-state relationship from telesis, the store of ontological potential. From the moment before this choice up to its 'actualization' or, equally, its incorporation into the telor's HCS, there occurs a process of 'telic attraction', that is, telesis in accordance with the telor's will is 'shaped' or molded into a syntax-state relationship of the telor's choosing. To quote Langan then: "Two features of conspansive spacetime, the atemporal homogeneity of IEDs (operator strata) y of extended superposition, then telic-recursively, coordinating events in such a way as to bring about its own emergence (subject to various more or less subtle restrictions involving available freedom, noise and competitive interference from other telons)". If these IEDS were not accessible, atemporally, via telic recursion—that is, if nomological strings only operated spatio-temporally—there would be no telic 'array' from which to choose compatible syntax-state relationships; the linear ectomorphic semimodel would cease to hold true to its very name, as there would be discrete jumps and spatio-temporal *and* nomological incompatibilities. In turn, this much would shatter the *consistency criterion* of God Himself.

6.13

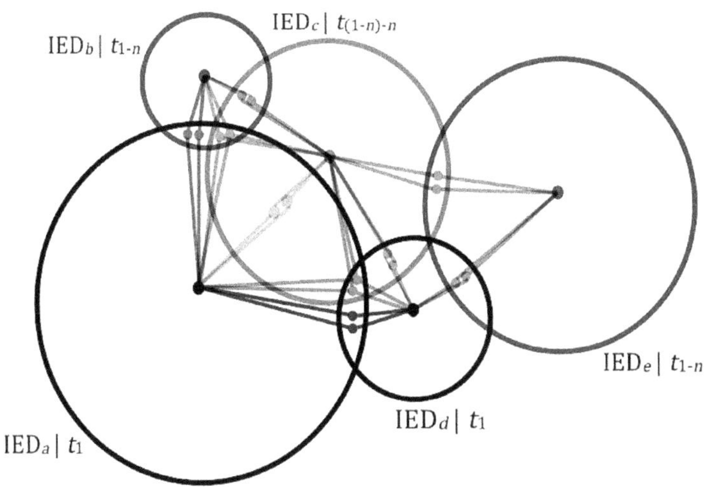

Spatially, inside any given IED, a telor can chose any point within (excluding for now permitted choices outside of the available IEDs), barring restrictions in the 'external world'—from tertiary syntactors or other secondary telons—that will prevent the telon, the chosen syntax-state relationship, from actualizing. Let's say that the above diagram represents IEDs of collections of objects of perception of a certain secondary telor. For IED*a*, the bottom left circle, it is in extended superposition with three other items of perception, IED_b, IED_c and IED_d. Let's say that, in the 'instant' of telic recursion after t_1, or the time *metasimultaneous* with the linear-ectomorphic output at t_2, the telor in question chooses an arrangement of syntax-state such that the *inner expanding* objects 'within' IED_a are shifted 3 arbitrary units to the left and 4 arbitrary units downwards (operating within 2 dimensions for simplicity) from where it was when the initial interaction between it and the object within IED_d occurred. Now, 'before' the choice is 'implemented' by the l-ectomorphic semimodel, the *telon* (syntax-state relationship) chosen by the telor 'adjusts' the *variant* portions of the telor's HCS (Human Cognitive Syntax) so as to bring about its existence. Here we get the sense in which Langan terms telons "pre-products"; in a pair of formal grammar production rules, $\{(ABa \rightarrow ACb), (ACb \rightarrow ABa)\}$, where the capitals are nonterminals and the lowers are terminals, '*ABa*' can be seen as the telon, as it produces a sort of 'bridge production', '*ACb*', so that it may 'transfer' itself from existence in the conspansive semimodel (Ls) to existence in the linear-ectomorphic semimodel (Lo), with its nonterminals, *A* and *B*, inside the telor as syntax and its terminal(s), *a* 'outside' the telor as state. Now, if the *relevant* syntaxes for the obtaining of the telon—the *cognitive* and *perceptual* syntaxes of the telor, the *nomological* sytntax generated by God, the physico- structural syntax of tertiary syntactors, the somatic- structural syntax of the telor, etc.—if these are such that nothing within them contradicts the telon, then said telon *will obtain*, barring any sort of direct interference by fellow telors.

6.131 To better understand the process of what Langan terms the "mutual acquisition" in the intersection of IEDs, we should further investigate the notion of *nested syntax*. For any item within reality, the invariant syntax of the Primary telor, in addition to other various syntaxes, rests *inside* this object, so that, in its evolution, it need not draw upon any syntax external to itself. For each collection of objects of the IEDs above, this syntax— while of course retaining its position inside the objects—gets *spatially expanded*, as its composite objects move about, carrying the endomorphic syntax outwards within the l-ectomorphic semimodel. While this spatial expansion of potential-acquisitional syntax is a key subprocess of the evolution of reality, the 'topology' of the syntax itself is an absolutely necessary precursor of this subprocess. Here we show a syndiffeonic diagram, showcasing the encapsulation of the diffeonic by the synetic. It is also important to ember that within each *d* reside more nested 'layers' of *s*.

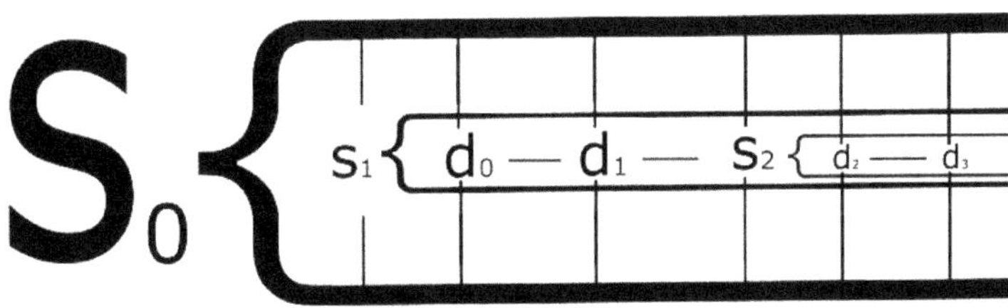

In terms of our previous IED diagram, we can see that, for each 'interaction' between the objects comprising a given IED, these objects were syntactically acquired by secondary telors, subjected to the given telor's or telors' HCSs. In the process of this syntactic acquisition, telic recursion, it is quite possible that multiple telors chose syntax-state relationships that implicated the very same objects. It is in this sense that tertiary syntactors can be simultaneously implicated in generalized-perceptual events—the atemporality of the IEDs and the subsequent possibility of *extended superposition* allows for such simultaneous integrations. For the given tertiary syntactor(s) implicated, their 'syntactic coverings' would differ at the level of HCS, while their Lo syntaxes, in addition to their Ls, non-HCS-related would be exactly the same.

6.2 As Langan states, secondary telors need not *directly* produce terminal strings; *secondary* telors can exist exclusively in the Ls semilanguage. Given that information transduction alone, via metacybernetic feedback, is a form of cognition, what Langan terms generalized cognition, entities with sufficient structural (syntactic) complexity for self-modeling need not produce their own terminals. What these strictly Ls- occupying telors can do is, through telons of the same syntax-state form of other telors', intelligently arrange the various syntaxes of the world.

6.21 It is possible that such Ls-confined telors 'emerge' from the mass interaction between terminal-producing telors in social and other cognitive processes. A 'group mind' is in this sense quite possible. Depending on the degree of separation from the symmetric MU form exhibited by the individual terminal-producing telors in question, there could be a certain degree of 'syntactic inertia', resulting in a deteriorating set of telors and, subsequently, differing properties/abilities of the group mind in question.

6.22 In terms of the formal grammar-based structure of what we have been discussing, we can provide a rough layout of the production rules involved, in addition to what Langan terms the 'modes' of production:

Telon for $a_x \in A$: $\{(ABa \rightarrow_{(GTR, LTR, IR)} ACb), (ACb \rightarrow_{(GTR, LTR, IR)} Aba)\}$

Nomological strings: $ab \rightarrow_{(GTR, IR)} cd$

Telic Principle (generalized utility): $A \rightarrow_{(GTR, LTR, IR)} B$

6.4 Telons of the Primary telor (God) can be such that they generate *syntactic* and *state-based* additions and alterations. For example, in terms of HCS (Human Cognitive Syntax), God can, by making additions to one's ETS (emo-telic syntax), induce certain feelings and sensations. He can of course make additions/alterations to other subcomponents of HCS as well. Although, as previously explained, He cannot directly interfere with a telor's choices via telic recursion.

6.41 Telons of God are items of the Will of God. There is reason to believe, and Langan has stated that these high-level telons are unknowable to us secondary telors. This is deeply intertwined with the P versus NP problem. Much more could be said on this in a specifically-geared analysis. Regardless of this, however, we can personally know God as an entity, as He is at all times within us, imbuing us with His syntax.

6.5 These propositions serve as rungs upon which to proudly and excitedly step, steadfastly continuing up to the ultimate conceptual viewing-point of Reality. As one climbs, one begins to realize that the rungs, and indeed the ladder itself, are melded with the world below. Not only this, but one grasps that he himself is connected to the ladder in much more than a physio-instrumental manner; he groks that he is, in some sense, creating this very tool that is enabling him to see that very fact! What once was a rather barren field lined with spatiotemporally distinct narrative is now seen to be a mutually-embracing, self-sustaining Reality of wonderous interconnection. *God is in man, and man is in God.*

7 Reality is a beautiful system, talking to Itself, about Itself, through only Itself.

www.ingramcontent.com/pod-product-compliance
Ingram Content Group UK Ltd.
Pitfield, Milton Keynes, MK11 3LW, UK
UKHW020138250726
13967UKWH00002B/725

9 781716 835292